**TEACHER'S PET PUBLICATIONS**

LITPLAN TEACHER PACK
for
Jane Eyre
based on the book by
Charlotte Brontë

Written by
Mary B. Collins

© 1996 Teacher's Pet Publications
All Rights Reserved

This **LitPlan** for Charlotte Bronte's
Jane Eyre
has been brought to you by Teacher's Pet Publications, Inc.

Copyright Teacher's Pet Publications 1996
11504 Hammock Point
Berlin MD 21811

Only the student materials in this unit plan
such as worksheets, study questions, assignment sheets, and tests
may be reproduced multiple times for use in the purchaser's classroom.

For any additional copyright questions,
contact Teacher's Pet Publications.

www.tpet.com

TABLE OF CONTENTS - *Jane Eyre*

Introduction	5
Unit Objectives	7
Reading Assignment Sheet	8
Unit Outline	9
Study Questions (Short Answer)	13
Quiz/Study Questions (Multiple Choice)	24
Pre-reading Vocabulary Worksheets	45
Lesson One (Introductory Lesson)	67
Nonfiction Assignment Sheet	69
Oral Reading Evaluation Form	71
Writing Assignment 1	75
Writing Assignment 2	85
Writing Assignment 3	87
Writing Evaluation Form	83
Vocabulary Review Activities	81
Extra Writing Assignments/Discussion ?s	79
Unit Review Activities	89
Unit Tests	93
Unit Resource Materials	127
Vocabulary Resource Materials	141

A FEW NOTES ABOUT THE AUTHOR
CHARLOTTE BRONTE

BRONTE FAMILY. The bleak, lonely moors of Yorkshire in England were the setting for two great novels of the 19th century. These were Charlotte Brontë's 'Jane Eyre' and Emily Brontë's 'Wuthering Heights'. Readers today are still enthralled by their tragic, romantic stories and by the sense of brooding mystery that shrouds the tales. The youngest sister, Anne, was also a talented novelist, and her books have the same haunting quality.

Their father was Patrick Brontë, a Church of England priest. Irish-born, he had changed his name from the more commonplace Brunty. After serving in several parishes he moved with his wife, Maria Branwell Brontë, and their six small children to Haworth in Yorkshire in 1820. Soon after, Mrs. Brontë, and the two eldest children died, leaving the father to care for the remaining three girls and a boy.

Charlotte, the eldest, was born in 1816. Emily was born in 1818 and Anne in 1820. Their brother Branwell was born in 1817. Left to themselves, the children wrote and told stories and walked over the desolate moors. They grew up largely self-educated. Branwell showed some talent for drawing. The girls determined to earn money for his art education. They took positions as teachers and governesses, but they were unhappy at being separated and away from Haworth.

To keep the family together, Charlotte planned to keep a school for girls at Haworth. She and Emily went to Brussels to learn foreign languages and school management. In 1844, using a small inheritance from an aunt, they prepared to open classes. Although they advertised, they received no pupils.

The failure of their venture left all the children at home. Branwell was unemployed. Temperamental and erratic, he turned to alcohol and opium. Charlotte again sought a way to help the family. She had found some of Emily's poems, written secretly, and realized their merit. She convinced her sisters they should publish a joint book of poems.

In 1846 the girls brought out at their own expense 'Poems by Currer, Ellis, and Acton Bell'. They chose masculine pen names but retained their own initials. Although critics liked the poems, only two volumes were sold. As children they had all written many stories. Charlotte, as a young girl, alone filled 22 volumes, each with 60 to 100 pages of minute handwriting. Again they turned to writing as a source of income.

'Jane Eyre' was immediately successful; the other two did not fare so well. Critics were hostile to 'Wuthering Heights'. They said it was too wild, too animallike. But silent, reserved Emily had put all her deep feelings into the book, and gradually it came to be considered one of the finest novels in the English language. Emily lived only a short while after the publication of her book, and Anne died in 1849.

Charlotte published 'Shirley' in 1849, and 'Villette' in 1853. She was acclaimed by London literary society, especially by William Makepeace Thackeray. In 1854 she married her father's curate, Arthur Bell Nicholls. But only a year later, she died of tuberculosis as her sisters had.

INTRODUCTION

This unit has been designed to develop students' reading, writing, thinking, and language skills through exercises and activities related to *Jane Eyre* by Charlotte Bronte. It includes twenty lessons, supported by extra resource materials.

Following the **introductory activity**, students are given a transition to explain how the activity relates to the book they are about to read. Following the transition, students are given the materials they will be using during the unit. At the end of the lesson, students begin the pre-reading work for the first reading assignment.

The **reading assignments** are approximately thirty pages each; some are a little shorter while others are a little longer. Students have approximately 15 minutes of pre-reading work to do prior to each reading assignment. This pre-reading work involves reviewing the study questions for the assignment and doing some vocabulary work for 8 to 10 vocabulary words they will encounter in their reading.

The **study guide questions** are fact-based questions; students can find the answers to these questions right in the text. These questions come in two formats: short answer or multiple choice. The best use of these materials is probably to use the short answer version of the questions as study guides for students (since answers will be more complete), and to use the multiple choice version for occasional quizzes. If your school has the appropriate equipment, it might be a good idea to make transparencies of your answer keys for the overhead projector.

The **vocabulary work** is intended to enrich students' vocabularies as well as to aid in the students' understanding of the book. Prior to each reading assignment, students will complete a two-part worksheet for approximately 8 to 10 vocabulary words in the upcoming reading assignment. Part I focuses on students' use of general knowledge and contextual clues by giving the sentence in which the word appears in the text. Students are then to write down what they think the words mean based on the words' usage. Part II nails down the definitions of the words by giving students dictionary definitions of the words and having students match the words to the correct definitions based on the words' contextual usage. Students should then have a thorough understanding of the words when they meet them in the text.

After each reading assignment, students will go back and formulate answers for the study guide questions. Discussion of these questions serves as a **review** of the most important events and ideas presented in the reading assignments.

After students complete reading the work, there is a lesson devoted to the **extra discussion questions/writing assignments**. These questions focus on interpretation, critical analysis and personal response, employing a variety of thinking skills and adding to the students' understanding of the novel.

Following the discussion questions, there is a **vocabulary review** lesson which pulls together all of the fragmented vocabulary lists for the reading assignments and gives students a review of all of the words they have studied.

The **group activity** which follows the vocabulary lesson has students working in small groups to discuss some of the novel's themes and ideas. Using the information they have acquired so far through individual work and class discussions, students get together to further examine the text and to brainstorm ideas relating to the themes of the novel.

The group activity is followed by a **reports and discussion** session in which the groups share their ideas about the themes with the entire class; thus, the entire class is exposed to information about all of the themes and the entire class can discuss each theme based on the nucleus of information brought forth by each of the groups.

There are three **writing assignments** in this unit, each with the purpose of informing, persuading, or having students express personal opinions. The first assignment is to express personal opinions: students give their own opinions about one of the main characters in the book (Rochester or Jane). The second assignment is to inform: students write a composition based on the information their group found in the group activity. The third assignment is to persuade: students write a persuasive argument defending their choice as the most important character in the book (other than Jane).

In addition, there is a **nonfiction reading assignment**. Students are required to read a piece of nonfiction related in some way to *Jane Eyre*. After reading their nonfiction pieces, students will fill out a worksheet on which they answer questions regarding facts, interpretation, criticism, and personal opinions. During one class period, students make **oral presentations** about the nonfiction pieces they have read. This not only exposes all students to a wealth of information, it also gives students the opportunity to practice **public speaking**.

The **review lesson** pulls together all of the aspects of the unit. The teacher is given four or five choices of activities or games to use which all serve the same basic function of reviewing all of the information presented in the unit.

The **unit test** comes in two formats: multiple choice or short answer. As a convenience, two different tests for each format have been included.

There are additional **support materials** included with this unit. The **extra activities section** includes suggestions for an in-class library, crossword and word search puzzles related to the novel, and extra vocabulary worksheets. There is a list of **bulletin board ideas** which gives the teacher suggestions for bulletin boards to go along with this unit. In addition, there is a list of **extra class activities** the teacher could choose from to enhance the unit or as a substitution for an exercise the teacher might feel is inappropriate for his/her class. **Answer keys** are located directly after the **reproducible student materials** throughout the unit. The student materials may be reproduced for use in the teacher's classroom without infringement of copyrights. No other portion of this unit may be reproduced without the written consent of Teacher's Pet Publications, Inc.

UNIT OBJECTIVES - *Jane Eyre*

1. Through reading *Jane Eyre*, students will study the themes of supernatural/dreams/visions, religion, education, and crime and punishment.

2. Students will study imagery and narrative techniques.

3. Students will compare and contrast characters to gain a better understanding of Charlotte Bronte's portraits of human nature.

4. Students will demonstrate their understanding of the text on four levels: factual, interpretive, critical and personal.

5. Students will be given the opportunity to practice reading aloud and silently to improve their skills in each area.

6. Students will answer questions to demonstrate their knowledge and understanding of the main events and characters in *Jane Eyre* as they relate to the author's theme development.

7. Students will enrich their vocabularies and improve their understanding of the novel through the vocabulary lessons prepared for use in conjunction with the novel.

8. The writing assignments in this unit are geared to several purposes:
    a. To have students demonstrate their abilities to inform, to persuade, or to express their own personal ideas

    > Note: Students will demonstrate ability to write effectively to <u>inform</u> by developing and organizing facts to convey information. Students will demonstrate the ability to write effectively to <u>persuade</u> by selecting and organizing relevant information, establishing an argumentative purpose, and by designing an appropriate strategy for an identified audience. Students will demonstrate the ability to write effectively to <u>express personal ideas</u> by selecting a form and its appropriate elements.

    b. To check the students' reading comprehension
    c. To make students think about the ideas presented by the novel
    d. To encourage logical thinking
    e. To provide an opportunity to practice good grammar and improve students' use of the English language.

9. Students will read aloud, report, and participate in large and small group discussions to improve their public speaking and personal interaction skills.

READING ASSIGNMENT SHEET - *Jane Eyre*

Date Assigned	Chapters Assigned	Completion Date
	1-6	
	7-11	
	12-16	
	17-19	
	20-23	
	24-26	
	27-29	
	30-33	
	34-38	

UNIT OUTLINE - *Jane Eyre*

1 Introduction PVR 1-6	2 Study ?s 1-6 PVR 7-11	3 Study ?s 7-11 PVR 12-16	4 Study ?s 12-16 PVR 17-19	5 Study?s 17-19 PVR 20-23 PVR 24-26
6 Writing Assignment 1	7 Quiz/?s 20-26 PVR 27-29	8 Library	9 Study ?s 27-29 PVR 30-33	10 Study ?s 30-33 Nonfiction Reports PVR 34-38
11 Study ?s 34-38 Extra ?s	12 Vocabulary	13 Group Activity	14 Discussion	15 Writing Assignment 2
16 Film	17 Film	18 Writing Assignment 3	19 Review	20 Test

Key: P = Preview Study Questions V = Prereading Vocabulary Work R = Read

STUDY GUIDE QUESTIONS

SHORT ANSWER STUDY GUIDE QUESTIONS - *Jane Eyre*

Chapters 1-6

1. How does Bronte immediately reveal Jane's situation to the reader?
2. Why do you think Jane is treated so unfairly?
3. What does Jane mean when she says she was "rather out of [her] self"?
4. On looking back, how does Jane understand Mrs. Reed's treatment of her?
5. Why does Mrs. Reed make Jane stay in the red room?
6. Why does Jane keep crying?
7. What hope does Mr. Lockwood give Jane?
8. How did Jane's character changed in her confrontation with both Mr. Brocklehurst and Mrs. Reed?
9. What is Lowood Institution?
10. What is the lifestyle of the girls at Lowood?
11. Why does Jane speak to the girl reading in the garden?
12. What advice does Helen give Jane?
13. How is Jane's temperament different from Helen's?

Chapters 7-11

1. Describe Mr. Brocklehurst.
2. How are Mr. Brocklehurst's wife and daughter dressed? What does that tell us?
3. How does Jane feel while standing on the stool when she is labeled a liar?
4. How does Helen comfort Jane?
5. Why does Miss Temple invite Jane to her room?
6. How does Jane's visit with Miss Temple alter her thinking about Lowood?
7. Who is Jane's new friend/schoolmate?
8. Where is Helen Burns?
9. Years after Helen's death, Jane has a stone marker with the word "Resurgam" carved upon it placed over Helen's grave. What is the significance of "Resurgam"?
10. What news does Bessie bring Jane from Gateshead?
11. What steps has Jane taken toward her future?
12. How does Jane find her position at Thornfield and her new acquaintances?

Chapters 12-16

1. What is Adele's relation to Mr. Rochester?
2. How does Jane first meet Mr. Rochester?
3. What is unusual about Jane's first meeting with Mr. Rochester?
4. Describe Mr. Rochester's appearance.
5. How does Mr. Rochester get a glimpse into Jane's nature and personality?
6. In what way does Jane captivate Mr. Rochester?
7. Why does Mr. Rochester bring up Adele when she is not his child?
8. After Jane saves Mr. Rochester from the fire, how do we know they are falling in love?
9. How does Jane respond to Grace Poole's composure when questioned about the fire?
10. How does Jane react to her feelings of love for Mr. Rochester?

Jane Eyre Short Answer Study Questions Page 2

Chapters 17-19
1. Contrast Blanche and Jane.
2. What does Jane perceive in the relationship between Blanche and Mr. Rochester?
3. Who is Mr. Mason?
4. How does Blanche react to her fortune?
5. What does Rochester the gypsy tell Blanche that upsets her?
6. What does the fortune teller tell Jane?
7. How does Mr. Rochester react to the news of Mason's arrival?

Chapters 20-23
1. What happens to Mason?
2. What does Jane do after Mr. Rochester calms everyone and sends them back to bed?
3. What does Mr. Rochester ask of Jane on the night before he is to be married?
4. Why does Jane consent to return to Gateshead?
5. How does Jane find the Reeds?
6. How do the Reeds treat Jane?
7. What does Mr. Rochester call Jane when he meets her on the road to Thornfield?
8. Jane is so happy to see Mr. Rochester that she lets down her guard; what does she tell him?
9. When Jane and Mr. Rochester profess their love and agree to marry, then a sudden storm breaks, resulting in lightening splitting the tree. What does nature reflect or foreshadow?

Chapters 24-26
1. Now that Jane is to become Mrs. Rochester, how does she act?
2. How does Mrs. Fairfax react to the announcement of Jane's marriage to Mr. Rochester?
3. What "vision" does Jane have the night before her wedding?
4. Who is Bertha?
5. Why were Jane and Mr. Rochester not married?

Chapters 27-29
1. What does Mr. Rochester ask of Jane?
2. Why can Jane not do as he asks?
3. What is Jane's answer to her dilemma?
4. What happens to Jane on her journey?
5. Who rescues Jane?
6. What name does Jane give the Rivers?
7. How do Diana and Mary treat Jane?

Jane Eyre Short Answer Study Questions Page 3

Chapters 30-33
 1. Describe Mary and Diana.
 2. Describe St. John.
 3. What employment does St. John find for Jane?
 4. Why does this employment suit Jane so much?
 5. Describe Jane's new home.
 6. How does Jane feel about her choice to leave Mr. Rochester?
 7. Identify Rosamond Oliver.
 8. What feelings does St. John have for Rosamond?
 9. Why is St. John correct in his rejection of Rosamond?
10. St. John and Jane both have strong wills; how are they different?

Chapters 34-38
1. What is St. John's offer to Jane, and why does she reject it?
2. How is St. John, although wishing to do good in the world, a villain?
3. What does Jane learn from the host at the inn in Millcote?
4. Contrast the manner in which St. John and Mr. Rochester seek to live.
5. How does the end of the novel represent typical Victorian expectations?

KEY: SHORT ANSWER STUDY GUIDE QUESTIONS - *Jane Eyre*

Chapters 1-6

1. How does Bronte immediately reveal Jane's situation to the reader?
    Before the end of the first page of the novel, we are aware Jane is excluded from the Reed family.

2. Why do you think Jane is treated so unfairly?
    She is obviously not a child of Mrs. Reed, and the lady dislikes her. The Reed children are spoiled and selfish and resent Jane's presence. They tease and abuse her cruelly and with impunity.

3. What does Jane mean when she says she was "rather out of [her] self"?
    Her defiance to unjust punishment occurs because she has nothing to lose. Once she releases her anger and frustration, she has some trouble controlling herself and only calms down under the threat of being tied down.

4. On looking back, how does Jane understand Mrs. Reed's treatment of her?
    She thinks if she had been a pretty child with a careless and romping nature, the Reeds could have been kind to her. Her temperament was not such that she could feel friendly towards the Reed children; she did not like them. She did not "fit in" to the family, and Mrs. Reed could not care for her.

5. Why does Mrs. Reed make Jane stay in the red room?
    She thinks Jane is trying to trick them into letting her out; she is repulsed by Jane's violence and supposed artifice.

6. Why does Jane keep crying?
    She does not see how she can ever escape her situation of abuse and cruelty.

7. What hope does Mr. Lockwood give Jane?
    He asks her if she would like to go to school.

8. How had Jane's character changed in her confrontation with both Mr. Brocklehurst and Mrs. Reed?
    Jane has found an inner resolve and an adult-like strength. She is not intimidated by either of them.

9. What is Lowood Institution?
    It is a charity school for orphaned girls.

10. What is the lifestyle of the girls at Lowood?
> They study the entire day with only a break for a walk in the garden. The food is poor, and their clothes are very plain. Only the barest necessities of life are provided for the girls there, but the standard of education is good.

11. Why does Jane speak to the girl reading in the garden?
> Because the girl sits alone and reads, Jane feels they are alike in their natures; Jane often found solace in books.

12. What advice does Helen give Jane?
> She tells Jane to endure criticism and punishment and to forgive and love her enemies.

13. How is Jane's temperament different from Helen's?
> Jane is a fighter who cannot meekly accept injustice.

Chapters 7-11

1. Describe Mr. Brocklehurst.
> He is an insensitive hypocrite. He orders that no extra food may be served if the porridge is burnt, asserting that fasting is better for the girls' souls. He also insists that the older girls must cut their hair to resist vanity and lust. He would have the girls living a most austere existence.

2. How are Mr. Brocklehurst's wife and daughter dressed? What does that tell us?
> They are wearing silks, furs, feathers and false curls. Their dress accentuates Mr. Brocklehurst's hypocrisy.

3. How does Jane feel while standing on the stool when she is labeled a liar?
> At first shame and indignation rise up in her, but then she perceives how the other girls react to her indignity. Helen smiles as she passes by Jane, and Jane takes courage from that and endures her punishment.

4. How does Helen comfort Jane?
> She tells her that Brocklehurst is not admired or liked by the girls and that if he had praised Jane the other girls would have been suspicious of her.

5. Why does Miss Temple invite Jane to her room?
> She wants to give Jane the opportunity to answer Brocklehurst's charges.

6. How does Jane's visit with Miss Temple alter her thinking about Lowood?
> Despite Lowood's deprivations, Jane begins to feel at home and with friends; she takes an interest in learning and sketching. For the first time in her life, Jane feels good about her future.

7. Who is Jane's new friend/schoolmate?
   Mary Ann Wilson is her new friend.

8. Where is Helen Burns?
   Helen becomes very ill with consumption (and eventually dies).

9. Years after Helen's death, Jane has a stone marker with the word "Resurgam" carved upon it placed over Helen's grave. What is the significance of "Resurgam"?
   "Resurgam" means "I shall rise again." Helen's deep faith insisted she would rise and live forever in heaven, and Jane's sense of justice demands it. The marker is a tribute to Helen and a kind of a command from Jane.

10. What news does Bessie bring Jane from Gateshead?
    Miss Eliza has spoiled Georgiana's elopement attempt, and they fight. John Reed spends too much money and leads a dissipated life. Bessie also tells Jane that a Mr. Eyre from Madeira came to see Jane, but he could not make the journey to Lowood because his ship was about to sail.

11. What steps has Jane taken toward her future?
    She has advertised for a position as a governess and is preparing to leave for Thornfield.

12. How does Jane find her position at Thornfield and her new acquaintances?
    She is very pleased at the kindness of Mrs. Fairfax and the beauty of the house.

Chapters 12-16
1. What is Adele's relation to Mr. Rochester?
   She is his ward.

2. How does Jane first meet Mr. Rochester?
   On the road from Hay, she meets a rider (we and she later find out is Mr. Rochester). She helps him return to his saddle after he and his horse go down on the ice.

3. What is unusual about Jane's first meeting with Mr. Rochester?
   Mr. Rochester does not tell Jane who he is.

4. Describe Mr. Rochester's appearance.
   He is a broad, square man. He is not tall. He has dark hair and a grim face. He is not handsome.

5. How does Mr. Rochester get a glimpse into Jane's nature and personality?
   He drills her with frank questions, which she answers with honesty and humor. She is obviously not to be outwitted by him. He also glimpses her wild, romantic inner nature through her paintings.

6. In what way does Jane captivate Mr. Rochester?
   He is charmed by her honesty and wit. She keeps a cool head during his "interrogations," giving him both sauciness and moral platitudes.

7. Why does Mr. Rochester bring up Adele when she is not his child?
   This shows Mr. Rochester to be a compassionate man. Even though Adele's mother scorned him, his treatment of them was not vindictive.

8. After Jane saves Mr. Rochester from the fire, how do we know they are falling in love?
   Mr. Rochester is reluctant to let go of her hand and murmurs that she struck his heart with delight when they first met. Also, that Mr. Rochester has spent so many weeks at Thornfield shows he enjoys the house more than he ever has before.

9. How does Jane respond to Grace Poole's composure when questioned about the fire?
   Jane is disturbed at Grace's calm matter-of-fact account of Rochester's "accident" since she is sure that Grace set the fire. She speculates that perhaps Grace and Mr. Rochester were once lovers but finds the idea ridiculous.

10. How does Jane react to her feelings of love for Mr. Rochester?
    She frankly evaluates her plainness and social position, especially upon hearing about the beautiful Blanche Ingram, whom Mr. Rochester admires. She decides that she has overreacted to Mr. Rochester's kindness and gratitude.

<u>Chapters 17-19</u>
1. Contrast Blanche and Jane.
   Blanche is beautiful, tall, and wealthy; Jane is plain, small, and poor. Blanche is well-versed in charming the gentlemen and playing the belle of the ball; Jane sits quietly and half-concealed in the window seat. Yet, it is clear that Blanche is shallow and cruel while Jane is kind and full of deep passions.

2. What does Jane perceive in the relationship between Blanche and Mr. Rochester?
   It is obvious to Jane that Blanche's flirtatious arrows always miss their mark and that Mr. Rochester does not love her. The jealousy Jane had begun to feel toward Blanche is replaced by a little pity for a woman trying too hard and unsuccessfully to charm.

3. Who is Mr. Mason?
   Mr. Mason is an old acquaintance of Mr. Rochester from the West Indies.

4. How does Blanche react to her fortune?
   She is not pleased; in fact, she seems rather distressed.

5. What does Rochester the gypsy tell Blanche that upsets her?
   He has hinted that Mr. Rochester is not as wealthy as she had thought he was.

6. What does the fortune teller tell Jane?
    She has happiness within her reach but her strong moral courage will prevent her from attaining it.

7. How does Mr. Rochester react to the news of Mason's arrival?
    He is extremely disturbed.

Chapters 20-23
1. What happens to Mason?
    He is stabbed and bitten during a midnight visit to the third story of Thornfield.

2. What does Jane do after Mr. Rochester calms everyone and sends them back to bed?
    She dresses and waits, thinking that Mr. Rochester will need her. (She has heard pleas from above her room that others could not have heard.)

3. What does Mr. Rochester ask of Jane on the night before he is to be married?
    He asks her to sit up with him.

4. Why does Jane consent to return to Gateshead?
    Mrs. Reed is dying and has asked for her. Jane must go because it is the moral thing to do; her conscience would not let her do otherwise. Besides, her feelings towards Mrs. Reed have changed and softened a bit with time.

5. How does Jane find the Reeds?
    Eliza is self-righteous and selfish; she spends her time on church and her account books. Georgiana is plump and spoiled, concerned only with finding a rich husband. John has killed himself after drinking and gambling away most of the family fortune.

6. How do the Reeds treat Jane?
    They do not welcome her although Eliza does admit that Jane seems to have a good head on her shoulders. The girls soften towards Jane a little when she promises to sketch them. Mrs. Reed is unchanged; she still dislikes Jane, but she does give Jane a three-year-old letter from John Eyre, who wishes to adopt Jane.

7. What does Mr. Rochester call Jane when he meets her on the road to Thornfield?
    He calls her an elf and a fairy.

8. Jane is so happy to see Mr. Rochester that she lets down her guard; what does she tell him?
    ". . . wherever you are is my home--my only home."

9. When Jane and Mr. Rochester profess their love and agree to marry, then a sudden storm breaks, resulting in lightning splitting the tree. What does nature reflect or foreshadow?
    Nature is a symbol that Jane and Mr. Rochester have a future unknown and stormy. The tree's splitting could symbolize the coming separation of Jane and Mr. Rochester, their "roots," their common bond, their love, still remaining.

Chapters 24-26

1. Now that Jane is to become Mrs. Rochester, how does she act?
    She remains the plain and simple governess and refuses to let Mr. Rochester adorn her in jewels and bright, colorful silks. She also must be firm and strict with Mr. Rochester since he has become giddy with happiness.

2. How does Mrs. Fairfax react to the announcement of Jane's marriage to Mr. Rochester?
    She half-heartedly congratulates Jane and warns her to beware and to proceed carefully.

3. What "vision" does Jane have the night before her wedding?
    A "ghost" dressed in white, with a disfigured face, came into her room and ripped her wedding veil in half.

4. Who is Bertha?
    Bertha is Mr. Rochester's wife. She is the one Grace Pool looks after in the third story of the house. She is the one who started the fire in Mr. Rochester's room. She is the one who appeared to Jane and ripped the veil. She is the one who attacked Mason.

5. Why were Jane and Mr. Rochester not married?
    Mr. Mason came to the church and accused Mr. Rochester of already being married. Mr. Rochester confessed and took everyone to the third floor to see Bertha.

Chapters 27-29

1. What does Mr. Rochester ask of Jane?
    He wants her to be his mistress.

2. Why can Jane not do as he asks?
    Her religious beliefs and her virtue will not allow her to succumb to what she knows and feels to be wrong.

3. What is Jane's answer to her dilemma?
    She decides she must leave Thornfield.

4. What happens to Jane on her journey?
   She pays all of her money for a ride away from Thornfield, and she leaves her bag in the coach by mistake. She has no money, no job, and has to go begging for food.

5. Who rescues Jane?
   St. John finds her on his doorstep and brings her into his house where he and his sisters care for her.

6. What name does Jane give the Rivers?
   She calls herself Jane Elliott.

7. How do Diana and Mary treat Jane?
   Both girls are very kind and friendly towards her.

Chapters 30-33

1. Describe Mary and Diana.
   The girls are both governesses and enjoy reading and the outdoors. Both are easygoing and friendly and find in Jane another sister.

2. Describe St. John.
   He is a parson who spends all his time tending to the poor and sick, yet he appears to have found no joy or peace in life.

3. What employment does St. John find for Jane?
   She will be the mistress of the new Morton school for girls.

4. Why does this employment suit Jane so much?
   It allows her more independence and respect.

5. Describe Jane's new home.
   Her home is a small cottage which is adequately furnished. It suits Jane.

6. How does Jane feel about her choice to leave Mr. Rochester?
   She is depressed and lonely, yet she believes the brief happiness she could have found as his mistress would have been overshadowed by her shame.

7. Identify Rosamond Oliver.
   She is the benefactress of Jane's school and a beautiful young lady of wealth who is in love with St. John.

8. What feelings does St. John have for Rosamond?
   He is attracted to her, but his resolute will refuses to allow him to swerve from his chosen path as a missionary.

9. Why is St. John correct in his rejection of Rosamond?
    Although he loves her, he realizes that his life's dream and hers do not converge. He desires to be a missionary more than he desires Rosamond, and he is certain she could never live as a missionary's wife.

10. St. John and Jane both have strong wills; how are they different?
    St. John is incapable of enjoying human feeling whereas Jane feels things very strongly. Jane is overjoyed more at finding a family than at receiving an inheritance, which puzzles St. John. His love for his sisters springs not from family and instinct but from respect and admiration. He calculates too much and cannot seem to allow himself to embrace human passions.

<u>Chapters 34-38</u>

1. What is St. John's offer to Jane, and why does she reject it?
    He wants her to come with him as his wife and companion missionary. She knows he does not love her as a spouse would, and she does not love him that way either. All he desires is a helper in his work, and he sees she has the qualities he seeks. Their marriage would, in his eyes, just be the convenience by which they could travel together.

2. How is St. John, although wishing to do good in the world, a villain?
    He tries to manipulate Jane by using religious ideals as blackmail. He desires to save the world, yet in achieving his goal to become a missionary, he shows a real selfishness and lack of concern for Jane. He appears to be ruthless in achieving his goal.

3. What does Jane learn from the host at the inn in Millcote?
    She learns that there was a fire at Thornfield. Bertha jumped from the roof to her death. She also learns that Mr. Rochester has lost his sight and a hand while attempting to save his insane wife from the fire.

4. Contrast the manner in which St. John and Mr. Rochester seek to live.
    Both men are searching for a meaningful life. Mr. Rochester spent his youthful search enjoying the joys of the flesh and the entertainments of the wealthy; his search led him to excess. St. John searches in the opposite direction; he renounces human passion and pleasant social intercourse for the Spartan life of a missionary in a foreign country. He looks for meaning in a life of duty and self-denial.

5. How does the end of the novel represent typical Victorian expectations?
    Those characters who did wrong must pay. Mrs. Reed suffered and died. Bertha dies violently. Rochester is maimed for his moral wrongs. Only due to his remorse and redemption is Mr. Rochester allowed happiness with Jane. Those characters who acted with goodness--Mrs. Fairfax, Diana, Mary and of course Jane--receive happiness and contentment for adhering to Christian virtues. St. John lived the life he wished for, one of hardship and self-sacrifice, and he finds his peace in his eternal reward.

MULTIPLE CHOICE STUDY GUIDE/QUIZ QUESTIONS - *Jane Eyre*

Chapters 1-6
1. True or False: Bronte reveals Jane's situation in the Reed household in a preface before the first chapter.
    A. True
    B. False

2. True or False: Jane is treated unfairly, probably because she was born during Mrs. Reed's first marriage, and she is a reminder to Mrs. Reed of her terrible mistake.
    A. True
    B. False

3. True or False: Jane defies the unjust punishment because she has nothing to lose. Once she releases the anger and frustration, she has some trouble controlling herself.
    A. True
    B. False

4. Which of the following statements does not describe Jane's understanding of Mrs. Reed's treatment of her?
    A. The Reeds would have been kinder had she (Jane) been prettier.
    B. Jane didn't like the Reed children.
    C. Jane didn't fit in with the family.
    D. Jane was too intelligent, which made Mrs. Reed feel that her own children were inferior. Mrs. Reed could not accept this and resented Jane.

5. True or False: Mrs. Reed makes Jane stay in the red room because she thinks red will have a calming effect on Jane.
    A. True
    B. False

6. True or False: Jane keeps crying because she doesn't see how she can ever escape her situation of cruelty and abuse.
    A. True
    B. False

7. What hope does Mr. Lockwood give Jane?
    A. He asks her if she would like to go into a convent.
    B. He asks her if she wants to go to America.
    C. He asks her if she wants to live with a different family.
    D. He asks her if she wants to go to school.

Jane Eyre Multiple Choice Study/Quiz Questions Page 2

8. True or False: During her confrontation with Mr. Brocklehurst and Mrs. Reed, Jane has found an inner resolve and adult-like strength. She is not intimidated by either of them.
   A. True
   B. False

9. What is Lowood Institution?
   A. It is a mental hospital.
   B. It is a prison.
   C. It is a charity school for orphaned girls.
   D. It is one of the few schools of higher learning that is open to women.

10. Which of the following does not describe the lifestyle of the residents of Lowood?
    A. They study the entire day with only a break for a walk in he garden.
    B. The food is poor.
    C. Their clothes are plain.
    D. The standard of education is poor.

11. Why does Jane speak to the girl reading in the garden?
    A. The girl spoke to her first.
    B. Jane feels they are alike in their natures because she also finds solace in books.
    C. Jane wants to borrow the book.
    D. The headmistress told her she had to speak to at least two people every day or risk expulsion: it is the headmistress' way of "socializing" Jane.

12. What advice does Helen give Jane?
    A. Be quiet but sneaky.
    B. Fight back at every opportunity.
    C. Endure punishment and criticism and forgive and love the enemy.
    D. Go along with the rules, read, and assimilate as much knowledge as possible: then escape.

13. How is Jane's temperament different from Helen's?
    A. Jane is more religious.
    B. Jane is not as neat and organized as Helen.
    C. Jane is shy, but Helen is not.
    D. Jane is a fighter who cannot meekly accept injustice.

Jane Eyre Multiple Choice Study/Quiz Questions Page 3

Chapters 7-11

1. Which of the following does not describe Mr. Brocklehurst?
    A. He says fasting is good for the girls' souls.
    B. He expects the girls to lead an austere life.
    C. He says the girls should never marry but should become governesses or teachers.
    D. He insists that the older girls cut their hair.

2. True or False: Mr. Brocklehurst's wife and daughters dress the way he insists that the girls in the school dress.
    A. True
    B. False

3. How does Jane feel while standing on the stool when she is labeled a liar?
    A. She feels triumphant.
    B. She feels isolated.
    C. She doesn't feel anything-she has gone numb.
    D. She takes courage from Helen and endures her punishment.

4. True or False: Helen comforts Jane by telling her that Brocklehurst is not admired or liked by the girls and that if he had praised Jane the other girls would have been suspicious of her.
    A. True
    B. False

5. Why does Miss Temple invite Jane to her room?
    A. She wants to punish Jane further.
    B. She wants Jane to clean for her.
    C. She wants to give Jane the opportunity to answer Brocklehurst's charges.
    D. She feels sorry for Jane and wants to befriend her.

6. How does Jane's visit with Miss Temple alter her thinking about Lowood?
    A. She begins to feel at home and with friends and feels good about her future.
    B. She dislikes it even more and feels even more depressed and hopeless.
    C. She looks at it as something that must be endured at all costs.
    D. She sees and understands the larger purpose of the school and appreciates what the administrators are trying to do--even if she doesn't like the way she is treated.

7. Who is Mary Ann Wilson?
    A. She is the new nurse.
    B. She is the headmistress sent to replace the one who was ill.
    C. She is Helen's benefactor.
    D. She is Jane's new friend/schoolmate.

Jane Eyre Multiple Choice Study/Quiz Questions Page 4

8. What happens to Helen Burns?
    A. She gets a teaching position and leaves the school.
    B. She is expelled for socializing with one of the delivery boys.
    C. She is ill with consumption and eventually dies.
    D. She enters a convent.

9. What is the significance of "Resurgam"?
    A. It was the girls' school motto: that they would always remember one another, and have a reunion every ten years.
    B. It was the word that Jane had engraved on the stone marker she placed on Helen's grave. It symbolized Helen's faith in the afterlife.
    C. It was part of a sermon that Brocklehurst gave to the girls every Sunday, reminding them that the consequences of their deeds, either good or bad, would follow them forever.
    D. It was a motivational message that Jane had made up for herself. Whenever she would get discouraged, she would remind herself that she had already come a long way and could do more.

10. Bessie visits Jane and brings news from Gateshead. Which of the following statements is not one of the news items?
    A. Miss Eliza has spoiled Georgiana's elopement attempt.
    B. John Reed spends too much money and leads a dissipated life.
    C. Mrs. Reed has a mysterious illness and is confined to her room.
    D. A Mr. Eyre from Madeira came to see her but could not make the journey to Lowood because his ship was about to sail.

11. What steps has Jane taken toward her future?
    A. She has applied to the university and hopes to receive a scholarship.
    B. She has learned to cook and hopes to become a chef.
    C. She has volunteered in the infirmary in the hopes of becoming a nurse's aide.
    D. She has advertised for a position as a governess and is preparing to leave for Thornfield.

12. How does Jane find her position at Thornfield and her new acquaintances?
    A. She doesn't like the people or the surroundings.
    B. She is pleased at the kindness of Mrs. Fairfax and the beauty of the house.
    C. She loves the peace and quiet she can find in the garden, but she detests her new acquaintances.
    D. She is disappointed in both the home and her new acquaintances.

Jane Eyre Multiple Choice Study/Quiz Questions Page 5

Chapters 12-16

1. What is Adele's relation to Mr. Rochester?
    A. She is his niece.
    B. She is his ward.
    C. She is his younger sister.
    D. She is his adopted daughter.

2. How does Jane first meet Mr. Rochester?
    A. She is introduced at dinner by the housekeeper.
    B. Mr. Rochester observes her teaching Adele. He later calls her into his office and introduces himself.
    C. Mr. Rochester picks her up at the station when she first arrives.
    D. She meets him on the road from Hay while she is out walking. She helps him return to his saddle after his horse goes down on the ice.

3. What is unusual about Jane's first meeting with Mr. Rochester?
    A. Mr. Rochester does not tell Jane who he is.
    B. Mr. Rochester does not speak to Jane. She thinks he is impaired.
    C. He acts as though he detests her.
    D. She feels an eerie chill, a premonition of something evil associated with him.

4. Which of the following statements does not describe Mr. Rochester's appearance?
    A. He is broad and square.
    B. He has dark hair.
    C. He is very tall.
    D. He has a grim face, and is not handsome.

5. How does Mr. Rochester get a glimpse into Jane's nature and personality?
    A. He sends for, and reads, her school records and the recommendations of her teachers.
    B. He observes her interacting with Adele and the household staff.
    C. He drills her with frank questions.
    D. He has her write an essay about her life.

6. In what way does Jane captivate Mr. Rochester?
    A. He is charmed by her honesty and wit.
    B. He thinks she is impudent and acts "above her station."
    C. He thinks she is a spoiled brat.
    D. He thinks she is too ignorant to hold the position she has undertaken.

Jane Eyre Multiple Choice Study/Quiz Questions Page 6

7. Why does Mr. Rochester bring up Adele when she is not his child?
   A. He feels guilty; he is not really sure that she is not his child.
   B. He is a compassionate man who was not vindictive even after Adele's mother scorned him.
   C. He secretly loves the little girl although he will not admit it.
   D. He thinks it makes him look generous and loving in the eyes of others.

8. True or False: After Jane saves Mr. Rochester from the fire, we (the readers) are able to surmise that they are falling in love.
   A. True
   B. False

9. How does Jane respond to Grace Poole's composure when questioned about the fire?
   A. She gets hysterical and accuses Grace of setting the fire.
   B. She is very calm and is not really affected by Grace's composure.
   C. She is disturbed at Grace's calm response since she is sure that Grace set the fire.
   D. She is afraid that Grace will do the same thing to her, so she stays in the background and acts as though it were an accident, caused by a fallen candle.

10. How does Jane react to her feelings of love for Mr. Rochester?
    A. She denies them because she can't bear to be hurt.
    B. She talks to Mrs. Fairfax, who reminds her that Mr. Rochester is far above her station in life.
    C. She gives in to her feelings and begins to plan ways to attract Mr. Rochester even more.
    D. She frankly evaluates her plainness and social position and decides she has overreacted to his kindness.

Jane Eyre Multiple Choice Study/Quiz Questions Page 7

Chapters 17-19
1. Which of the following statements does not describe Blanche Ingram?
    A. She is kind and full of deep passions.
    B. She is tall and beautiful.
    C. She is well-versed in charming the gentlemen.
    D. She is very wealthy.

2. What does Jane perceive in the relationship between Blanche and Mr. Rochester?
    A. She sees that they are deeply in love.
    B. She sees that Mr. Rochester loves Blanche, but she does not love him.
    C. She sees that Blanche's flirtatious arrows miss their mark, and Mr. Rochester does not love her.
    D. She sees that they both really despise the other but are playing the courting game for amusement.

3. Who is Mr. Mason?
    A. He is Mr. Rochester's cousin.
    B. He is an old acquaintance of Mr. Rochester from the West Indies.
    C. He is Mr. Rochester's lawyer.
    D. He is a fortune teller and magician whom Mr. Rochester has hired for entertainment.

4. How does Blanche react to her fortune?
    A. She does not believe in it at all: she was merely playing along to keep the party atmosphere.
    B. She is angry that Mr. Rochester let the fortune teller in because she is a very strict Christian.
    C. She chooses the parts she wants to believe are true and discards the rest.
    D. She is not please; in fact, she seems rather distressed.

5. What does Rochester the gypsy tell Blanche?
    A. He says she will have a long life but will not always be happy.
    B. He says she will never marry although she will have many suitors.
    C. He says she will die young of a terrible disease.
    D. He hints that Mr. Rochester is not as wealthy as she had thought he was.

Jane Eyre Multiple Choice Study/Quiz Questions Page 8

6. True or False: The fortune teller tells Jane she will become happy and wealthy in a short time.
    A. True
    B. False

7. How does Mr. Rochester react to the news of the Mason's arrival?
    A. He is very pleased.
    B. He is neutral.
    C. He is very disturbed.
    D. He leaves.

Jane Eyre Multiple Choice Study/Quiz Questions Page 9

<u>Chapters 20-23</u>
1. What happens to Mason?
    A. He falls in love with Blanche Ingram.
    B. He has a terrible fight with Mr. Rochester and is asked to leave the estate.
    C. He becomes very ill and Jane nurses him back to health.
    D. He is stabbed and bitten during a midnight visit to the third story of Thornfield.

2. What does Jane do after Mr. Rochester calms everyone and sends them to bed?
    A. She packs her bag and gets ready to leave the next morning.
    B. She trembles, hides under the covers, and bolts her door.
    C. She dresses and waits in case Mr. Rochester needs her.
    D. She goes in to sleep with Adele to make sure she is safe.

3. What does Mr. Rochester ask of Jane on the night before he is to be married?
    A. He asks her to sit up with him.
    B. He asks her to pack his trunk.
    C. He asks her to have dinner with him.
    D. He asks her to stay in her room and not be seen.

4. Why does Jane consent to return to Gateshead?
    A. Mr. Rochester tells her she must do it or she cannot stay at Thornfield.
    B. She knows it is the moral thing to do.
    C. She secretly hopes she will receive a portion of Mrs. Reed's fortune if she is kind and compassionate.
    D. She is merely curious about what all of the family members have been doing.

5. Which of the following does not describe the way Jane finds the Reeds?
    A. Mrs. Reed is dying.
    B. Eliza is self-righteous and selfish and spends her time on church and her account book.
    C. Georgianna is plump and spoiled and is only concerned with looking for a rich husband.
    D. John, while being a drinker and gambler, has managed to increase the family fortune several times over.

6. How do the Reeds treat Jane?
    A. They do not welcome her, as they still dislike her.
    B. They have softened and are warm and friendly.
    C. They act as if they have never seen her before.
    D. They shower gifts upon her to make up for their years of tyranny.

Jane Eyre Multiple Choice Study/Quiz Questions Page 10

7. What does Mr. Rochester call Jane when he meets her on the road to Thornfield.
    A. He calls her angel.
    B. He calls her precious gem.
    C. He calls her an elf and a fairy.
    D. He calls her a goddess.

8. What does Jane tell Mr. Rochester?
    A. She missed him but was glad for the change of pace.
    B. She wants to leave and try her luck in the world.
    C. She wants to go to school.
    D. Her only home is with him.

9. When Jane and Mr. Rochester profess their love and agree to marry, a sudden storm breaks out. The resulting lightening splits the tree. What is this literary device called?
    A. Simile
    B. Personification
    C. Foreshadowing
    D. Transcendentalism

Jane Eyre Multiple Choice Study/Quiz Questions Page 11

<u>Chapters 24-26</u>
1. Now that Jane is to become Mrs. Rochester, how does she act?
    A. She becomes joyful and impulsive, and laughs and sings.
    B. She remains the plain and simple governess and is firm and strict with Mr. Rochester.
    C. She is nervous and cries a lot.
    D. She suddenly becomes very arrogant, and begins to order the others around.

2. How does Mrs. Fairfax react to the announcement of Jane's marriage to Mr. Rochester?
    A. She is delighted, and wishes them both happiness.
    B. She is very angry, and scolds Jane for marrying above her station.
    C. She is upset, because she is afraid she will lose her job if Jane doesn't like her. She becomes excessively subservient to Jane.
    D. She halfheartedly congratulates her and warns her to beware, and proceed carefully.

3. What "vision" does Jane have the night before the wedding?
    A. A ghost dressed in white, with a disfigured face, came into her room and ripped the wedding veil in half.
    B. The carriage overturned on the way to the church and she and Mr. Rochester were trapped under it.
    C. Thornfield was on fire and she was trapped upstairs.
    D. The church crumbled and fell apart just as they were ready to take their vows.

4. Who is guilty of setting the fire, ripping Jane's veil, and attacking Mason?
    A. Grace Poole. She is madly in love with Mr. Rochester, and will stop at nothing to have him.
    B. Mr. Rochester did it himself. He has fits of anger, and doesn't remember what happened after he comes out of the fits.
    C. Mr. Rochester's insane wife, Bertha, committed all of the acts.
    D. Mrs. Fairfax is guilty. She believed she could save Jane if she frightened her away from Mr. Rochester.

5. True or False: Jane and Mr. Rochester were not married because Mr. Mason came to the church and accused Mr. Rochester of already being married.
    A. True
    B. False

Jane Eyre Multiple Choice Study/Quiz Questions Page 12

Chapters 27-29

1. What does Mr. Rochester ask of Jane?
    A. He wants her to leave Thornfield.
    B. He wants her to be his mistress.
    C. He wants her to care for Bertha.
    D. He wants her to stay on as Adele's governess and go on as though nothing had happened.

2. What is Jane's answer to his question?
    A. She says yes.
    B. She says no.
    C. She puts him off until an indefinite date in the future.
    D. She just laughs at him.

3. What is Jane's answer to her dilemma?
    A. She decides she should leave Thornfield.
    B. She decides to stay because she has no where else to go.
    C. She decides to go back to school to further her own education.
    D. She decides to become a nun.

4. Which does not happen to Jane on her journey?
    A. She becomes ill and is hospitalized.
    B. She pays all of her money for a ride away from Thornfield.
    C. She leaves her bag in the coach by mistake.
    D. She has to go begging for food.

5. Who rescues Jane?
    A. The village clergyman rescues her.
    B. Diana and Mary find her in the woods and bring her home with them.
    C. The woman from the bread shop takes her in.
    D. St. John finds her on his doorstep and takes her in.

6. What name does Jane give the Rivers?
    A. She calls herself Jane Rochester.
    B. She gives her real name, Jane Eyre.
    C. She calls herself Jane Reed.
    D. She calls herself Jane Elliott.

Jane Eyre Multiple Choice Study/Quiz Questions Page 13

7. How do Diana and Mary treat Jane?
    A. They are as mean as the Reed sisters were.
    B. Diana is friendly, but Mary is suspicious.
    C. They are both kind and friendly.
    D. Mary is very friendly, but Diana is stand-offish.

Jane Eyre Multiple Choice Study/Quiz Questions Page 14

Chapters 30-33

1. Which of the following statements does not describe Mary and Diana?
    A. They are both great beauties.
    B. They enjoy reading.
    C. They are easy-going and friendly.
    D. They enjoy the outdoors.

2. Describe St. John.
    A. He is wild and untamed.
    B. He is highly intellectual and has little thought for material things.
    C. He spends all of his time tending to the poor and sick, yet he appears to have found no peace or joy in life.
    D. He is very romantic although he usually manages to keep that side of himself hidden.

3. What employment does St. John find for Jane?
    A. She will take care of a wealthy invalid woman in the town.
    B. She will be the housekeeper for the church.
    C. She will be a dressmaker's assistant.
    D. She will be the mistress of the new Morton school for girls.

4. Does this employment suit Jane?
    A. No, it doesn't. It reminds her too much of her former life, and the pay is very low.
    B. Yes, it does. It allows her more independence and respect.

5. Describe Jane's new home.
    A. It is a corner in the far end of the room. It is barely livable.
    B. It is a lavish apartment, and she is not accustomed to such comfort.
    C. It is a cold, run-down shack, but she thinks she will be able to make the best of it.
    D. It is a small cottage, already furnished.

6. True or False: Although Jane is depressed and lonely about her choice to leave Mr. Rochester, she believes that any happiness she could have had as his mistress would have been overshadowed by her shame.
    A. True
    B. False

7. Which of the following statements does not describe Rosamond Oliver?
    A. She is the benefactress of the school.
    B. She is in love with St. John.
    C. She is the daughter of the vicar of the shire.
    D. She is beautiful and wealthy.

Jane Eyre Multiple Choice Study/Quiz Questions Page 15

8. What feelings does St. John have for Rosamond?
    A. He is not interested in her at all.
    B. He is attracted, but his resolute will refuses to allow him to swerve from his chosen path as a missionary.
    C. He is interested and is having a conflict over whether or not to pursue her.
    D. He only has feelings of resentment for her.

9. How does the author portray St. John's decision regarding Rosamond?
    A. He is correct in his rejection of her because their life dreams do not converge.
    B. He is making a foolish mistake because of his overly-zealous sense of mission.
    C. He is too concerned over the decision itself; it doesn't matter what the decision *is*, just as long as he makes a decision.
    D. He is acting too rashly and needs to consider the issue more carefully.

10. True or False: St. John and Jane are both capable of very strong feelings.
    A. True
    B. False

11. True or False: Jane is more overjoyed at finding a family than in receiving an inheritance.
    A. True
    B. False

12. St. John is very calculating and cannot seem to allow himself to embrace human passions.
    A. True
    B. False

Jane Eyre Multiple Choice Study/Quiz Questions Page 16

Chapters 34-38

1. What is St. John's offer to Jane?
    A. He wants her to start a missionary church in Ireland.
    B. He wants her to take over the running of Moor House and open it as an orphanage.
    C. He wants to send her to school, all expenses paid.
    D. He wants her to come with him as his wife and companion missionary.

2. What is Jane's answer to his offer?
    A. She accepts it.
    B. She rejects it.

3. True or False: The author portrays St. John as a villain. Although he wishes to do good in the world, he is using his religious ideals as blackmail.
    A. True
    B. False

4. What does Jane learn from the host at the inn in Millcote?
    A. Mr. Rochester has gone to live in Australia. He has left Bertha at Thornfield in the care of Mrs. Poole.
    B. Mr. Rochester has a mistress whom he has housed on an estate close to Thornfield.
    C. There was a fire at Thornfield. Bertha jumped to her death, and Mr. Rochester lost his sight and one hand in attempting to rescue her.
    D. Mr. Rochester has lost his money in some bad business dealings. He is living with Mr. Mason. Bertha has been sent to an asylum.

5. Identify the character who is being described: His/her youth was spent enjoying the joys of the flesh and the entertainments of the wealthy; this leads to excesses.
    A. It was St. John Eyre Rivers.
    B. It is Mr. Rochester.
    C. It is Mr. Mason.
    D. It is Bertha Mason.

6. Which character in the novel looked for a meaning in a life of duty and self-denial?
    A. It was Jane Eyre.
    B. It was Mrs. Poole.
    C. It was Mr. Brocklehurst.
    D. It was St. John Rivers.

Jane Eyre Multiple Choice Study/Quiz Questions Page 17

7. The novel's conclusion is typical of the period: characters who did wrong must pay, those who acted with goodness are rewarded. What is the name of this period or style of writing?
    A. It is the Classical style.
    B. It is Realistic Fiction.
    C. It is the Victorian style.
    D. It is a tragedy.

ANSWER KEY - MULTIPLE CHOICE STUDY/QUIZ QUESTIONS
Jane Eyre

Chapters 1-6	Chapters 7-11	Chapters 12-16	Chapters 17-19
1. B	1. C	1. B	1. A
2. B	2. B	2. D	2. C
3. A	3. D	3. A	3. B
4. D	4. A	4. C	4. D
5. B	5. C	5. C	5. D
6. A	6. A	6. A	6. B
7. D	7. D	7. B	7. C
8. A	8. C	8. A	
9. C	9. B	9. C	
10. D	10. C	10. D	
11. B	11. D		
12. C	12. B		
13. D			

Chapters 20-23	Chapters 24-26	Chapters 27-29	Chapters 30-33
1. D	1. B	1. B	1. A
2. C	2. D	2. B	2. C
3. A	3. A	3. A	3. D
4. B	4. C	4. A	4. B
5. D	5. A	5. D	5. D
6. A		6. D	6. A
7. C		7. C	7. C
8. D			8. B
9. C			9. A
			10. B
			11. A
			12. A

Chapters 34-38
1. D
2. B
3. A
4. C
5. B
6. D
7. C

PREREADING VOCABULARY WORKSHEETS

VOCABULARY - *Jane Eyre*

Chapters 1 - 6 Part I: Using Prior Knowledge and Contextual Clues

Below are the sentences in which the vocabulary words appear in the text. Read the sentence. Use any clues you can find in the sentence combined with your prior knowledge, and write what you think the underlined words mean on the lines provided.

1. John Reed was a schoolboy of fourteen years old; . . . . .with a dingy and unwholesome skin; thick lineaments in a spacious <u>visage</u>, heavy limbs and large extremities.

    _____

2. This preparation for bonds, and the additional <u>ignominy</u> it inferred, took a little of the excitement out of me.

    _____

3. "What is all this?" demanded another voice <u>peremptorily</u>; and Mrs. Reed came along the corridor, her cap flying wide, her gown rustling stormily.

    _____

4. Fearful, however, of losing this first and only opportunity of relieving my grief by imparting it, I, after a disturbed pause, contrived to frame a <u>meager</u>, though, as far as it went, true response.

    _____

5. . . . but as I instantly turned against him, roused by the same sentiment of deep ire and desperate revolt which had stirred my corruption before, he thought it better to desist, and ran from me uttering <u>execrations</u>, and vowing I had burst his nose.

    _____

6. That eye of hers, that voice stirred every <u>antipathy</u> I had.

    _____

7. I would <u>fain</u> exercise some better faculty than that of fierce speaking; fain find nourishment for some less fiendish feeling than that of somber indignation.

    _____

Vocabulary - *Jane Eyre* - Chapters 1 - 6 Continued

8. Not a tear rose to Burns' eye; and, while I paused from my sewing, because my fingers quivered at this spectacle with a sentiment of unavailing and impotent anger, not a feature of her pensive face altered its ordinary expression.

_____

9. . . . I was wondering how a man who wished to do right could act so unjustly and unwisely as Charles the First sometimes did; and I thought what a pity it was that, with his integrity and conscientiousness, he could see no farther than the prerogatives of the crown.

_____

10. We are. . . . .burdened with faults in this world: but the time will soon come . . . when debasement and sin will fall from us with this cumbrous frame of flesh, and only the spark of the spirit will remain,--the impalpable principle of life and thought, pure as when it left the Creator to inspire the creature: whence it came it will return. . . .

_____

Part II: Determining the Meaning
    Match the vocabulary words to their dictionary definitions. If there are words for which you cannot figure out the definition by contextual clues and by process of elimination, look them up in a dictionary.

___ 1. visage   A. disgrace; dishonor; public contempt; base conduct
___ 2. ignominy   B. instinctive opposition; natural dislike; aversion
___ 3. peremptorily   C. prior or exclusive rights or privileges
___ 4. meagre   D. the face; appearance
___ 5. execrations   E. intangible; cannot be readily grasped by the mind
___ 6. antipathy   F. lean; deficient in quantity or quality
___ 7. fain   G. curses; utterances of detestation
___ 8. pensive   H. positive in speech, tone, manner, etc.; dictatorial
___ 9. prerogatives   I. willingly; gladly; by preference
___ 10. impalpable   J. deeply, seriously or sadly thoughtful; melancholy

Vocabulary - *Jane Eyre* Chapters 7 - 11

Part I: Using Prior Knowledge and Contextual Clues

Below are the sentences in which the vocabulary words appear in the text. Read the sentence. Use any clues you can find in the sentence combined with your prior knowledge, and write what you think the underlined words mean on the lines provided.

1. A little solace came at tea-time, in the shape of a double ration of bread---a whole, instead of a half, slice---with the delicious addition of a thin scrape of butter: it was the hebdomadal treat to which we all looked forward from Sabbath to Sabbath.

_____

2. I had my own reasons for being dismayed at this apparition: too well I remembered the perfidious hints given by Mrs. Reed about my disposition, etc.; the promise pledged by Mr. Brocklehurst to apprise Miss Temple and the teachers of my vicious nature.

_____

3. . . . I did not doubt he was making disclosures of my villainy; and I watched her eye with painful anxiety, expecting every moment to see its dark orb turn on me a glance of repugnance and contempt.

_____

4. Should any little accidental disappointment of the appetite occur, such as the spoiling of a meal,. . . . . . . it ought to be improved to the spiritual edification of the pupils, by encouraging them to evince fortitude under the temporary privation.

_____

5. "I know something of Mr. Lloyd; I shall write to him; if his reply agrees with your statement, you shall be publicly cleared from every imputation; to me, Jane, you are clear now."

_____

6. Spring drew on, she was indeed already come; the frosts of winter had ceased; its snows were melted, its cutting winds ameliorated.

_____

Vocabulary - *Jane Eyre* - Chapters 7 - 11 Continued

7. I had <u>imbibed</u> from her something of her nature and much of her habits: . . . .

_____

8. . . . he was a clergyman, <u>incumbent</u> of Hay---that little village yonder on the hill---and that church near the gates was his.

_____

Part II: Determining the Meaning

Match the vocabulary words to their dictionary definitions. If there are words for which you cannot figure out the definition by contextual clues and by process of elimination, look them up in a dictionary.

___ 11. solace
___ 12. perfidious
___ 13. orb
___ 14. edification
___ 15. imputation
___ 16. ameliorated
___ 17. imbibed
___ 18. incumbent

A. improved
B. circular; the eye; a sphere
C. drank; absorbed or taken in as if by drinking
D. basely treacherous; deliberately faithless
E. holder of an office; one who holds an ecclesiastical benefice; obligatory
F. something that gives comfort, consolation or relief
G. instruction in moral improvement or benefit
H. a charge or insinuation of something discreditable

Vocabulary - *Jane Eyre* - Chapters 12 - 16

Part I: Using Prior Knowledge and Contextual Clues

Below are the sentences in which the vocabulary words appear in the text. Read the sentence. Use any clues you can find in the sentence combined with your prior knowledge, and write what you think the underlined words mean on the lines provided.

1. "The governess!" and again my raiment underwent scrutiny.

_____

2. She hastened to ring the bell; and, when the tray came, she proceeded to arrange the cups, spoons, etc., with assiduous celerity.

_____

3. . . . he would sometimes pass me haughtily and coldly, just acknowledging my presence by a distant nod or a cool glance, and sometimes bow and smile with gentlemanlike affability.

_____

4. " . . . I have forbidden Adele to talk to me about her presents, and she is bursting with repletion; have the goodness to serve her as auditress and interlocutrice: it will be one of the most benevolent acts you ever performed."

_____

5. "Leaving superiority out of the question then, you must still agree to receive my orders now and then, without being piqued or hurt by the tone of command---will you?"

_____

6. "Yes, yes, you are right," he said; "I have plenty of faults of my own: I know it, and I don't wish to palliate them, I assure you."

_____

7. "Ah! in that case I must abridge."

_____

Vocabulary - *Jane Eyre* - Chapters 12 - 16 Continued

8. . . . but there was something decidedly strange in the <u>paroxysm</u> of emotion which had suddenly seized him, when he was in the act of expressing the present contentment of his mood, and his newly revived pleasure in the old hall and its environs.

_____

9. I rushed to his basin and <u>ewer</u>; fortunately one was wide and the other deep, and both were filled with water.

_____

10. To much <u>confabulation</u> succeeded a sound of scrubbing and setting to rights; and when I passed the room. . . . .I saw through the open door that all was again restored to complete order; only the bed was stripped of its hangings.

_____

Part II: Determining the Meaning

Match the vocabulary words to their dictionary definitions. If there are words for which you cannot figure out the definition by contextual clues and by process of elimination, look them up in a dictionary.

___ 19. raiment
___ 20. assiduous
___ 21. affability
___ 22. repletion
___ 23. piqued
___ 24. palliate
___ 25. abridge
___ 26. paroxysm
___ 27. ewer
___ 28. confabulation

A. to disguise or conceal; excuse
B. easy of conversation or approach
C. a pitcher
D. wounded pride or self-esteem; resentment
E. a chat; talking together
F. clothing
G. sudden, violent outburst; a convulsion; fit of emotion
H. devoted; unremittingly attentive; constant in application
I. omit; shorten; curtail; deprive of
J. condition of being filled up with something

Vocabulary - *Jane Eyre* - Chapters 17 - 19

Part I: Using Prior Knowledge and Contextual Clues

Below are the sentences in which the vocabulary words appear in the text. Read the sentence. Use any clues you can find in the sentence combined with your prior knowledge, and write what you think the underlined words mean on the lines provided.

1. From school duties she was <u>exonerated</u>: Mrs. Fairfax had pressed me into her service, and I was all day in the store-room, helping (or hindering) her and the cook; . . . .

_____

2. ". . . and he replied in his quick way: 'Nonsense! If she objects, tell her it is my particular wish; and if she resists, say I shall come and fetch her in case of <u>contumacy</u>.' "

_____

3. And then they had called her to a sofa, where she now sat, <u>ensconced</u> between them, chattering alternately in French and broken English; . . . . . .

_____

4. "My dearest, don't mention governesses; the word makes me nervous. I have suffered a martyrdom from their incompetency and <u>caprice</u>; I thank Heaven I have now done with them!"

_____

5, 6, & 7. Too often she betrayed this, by the undue vent she gave to a spiteful antipathy she had conceived against little Adele: pushing her away with some <u>contumelious</u> <u>epithet</u> if she happened to approach her; sometimes ordering her from the room, and always treating her with coldness and <u>acrimony</u>.

_____

_____

_____

Vocabulary - *Jane Eyre* - Chapters 17 - 19 Continued

8. Arrows. . . might, I knew, if shot by a surer hand, have quivered keen in his proud heart—have called love into his stern eye, and softness into his <u>sardonic</u> face: or, better still, without weapons a silent conquest might have been won.

_____

9. I don't understand <u>enigmas</u>.

_____

10. I need not sell my soul to buy <u>bliss</u>.

_____

Part II: Determining the Meaning

Match the vocabulary words to their dictionary definitions. If there are words for which you cannot figure out the definition by contextual clues and by process of elimination, look them up in a dictionary.

___ 29. exonerated A. bitter; scornful or mocking
___ 30. contumacy B. settled securely or snugly
___ 31. ensconced C. riddles; puzzles; mysteries
___ 32. caprice D. relieved from an obligation, duty or task; freedom from blame
___ 33. contumelious E. a whim; mere fancy; sudden change of mind
___ 34. epithet F. supreme happiness
___ 35. acrimony G. irritating or angry sharpness
___ 36. sardonic H. humiliatingly insolent
___ 37. enigmas I. a name; an adjective or term applied to a person or thing to express an attribute; a phrase or expression
___ 38. bliss J. willful and obstinate resistance or disobedience

Vocabulary - *Jane Eyre* - Chapters 20 - 23

Part I: Using Prior Knowledge and Contextual Clues
Below are the sentences in which the vocabulary words appear in the text. Read the sentence. Use any clues you can find in the sentence combined with your prior knowledge, and write what you think the underlined words mean on the lines provided.

1. Indeed, whatever being uttered that fearful shriek could not soon repeat it: not the widest-winged condor on the Andes could, twice in succession, send out such a yell from the cloud shrouding his <u>eyrie</u>.

   _____

2 & 3. What crime was this, that lived <u>incarnate</u> in the <u>sequestered</u> mansion, and could neither be expelled nor subdued by the owner?

   _____

   _____

4. <u>Presentiments</u> are strange things!

   _____

5. I did not like this <u>iteration</u> of one idea---this strange recurrence of one image; and I grew nervous as bedtime approached and the hour of the vision drew near.

   _____

6. . . . and she placed before me a little round stand with my cup and a plate of toast, absolutely as she used to accommodate me with some privately <u>purloined</u> dainty on a nursery chair: and I smiled and obeyed her as in bygone days.

   _____

7. There was something <u>ascetic</u> in her look, which was augmented by the extreme plainness of a straight-skirted, black, stiff dress, a starched linen collar, hair combed away from the temples, and the nun-like ornament of a string of ebony beads and a crucifix.

   _____

Vocabulary - *Jane Eyre* - Chapters 20 - 23 Continued

8. A sneer, however, whether <u>covert</u> or open, had now no longer that power over me it once possessed: . . . .

_____

9. . . . I had left this woman with bitterness and hate, and I came back to her now with no other emotion than a sort of <u>ruth</u> for her great sufferings, and a strong yearning to forget and forgive all injuries---to be reconciled and clasp hands in amity.

_____

10. Eliza generally took no more notice of her sister's <u>indolence</u> and complaints than if no such murmuring, lounging object had been before her.

_____

Part II: Determining the Meaning
    Match the vocabulary words to their dictionary definitions. If there are words for which you cannot figure out the definition by contextual clues and by process of elimination, look them up in a dictionary.

    ____ 39. eyrie   A. repetition
    ____ 40. incarnate   B. secluded or out-of-the-way, as places; withdrawn from others
    ____ 41. sequestered   C. laziness
    ____ 42. presentiments D. to embody in flesh; to represent in a concrete way
    ____ 43. iteration   E. sorrow; regret; pity or compassion
    ____ 44. purloined   F. nest of a bird of prey; any nest, habitation or position of loft
    ____ 45. ascetic   G. stolen; done away with
    ____ 46. covert   H. forebodings; a feeling that something is going to happen
    ____ 47. ruth   I. one who practices religious austerities; a hermit or recluse
    ____ 48. indolence   J. disguised; secret; concealed

Vocabulary - *Jane Eyre* - Chapters 24 - 26

Part I: Using Prior Knowledge and Contextual Clues

Below are the sentences in which the vocabulary words appear in the text. Read the sentence. Use any clues you can find in the sentence combined with your prior knowledge, and write what you think the underlined words mean on the lines provided.

1. Mr. Rochester had sometimes read my unspoken thoughts with an <u>acumen</u> to me incomprehensible: in the present instance he took no notice of my abrupt vocal response; but he smiled at me with a certain smile he had of his own, and which he used but on rare occasions.

   _____

2. I did not like to walk at this hour alone with Mr. Rochester in the shadowy orchard; but I could not find a reason to <u>allege</u> to leave him.

   _____

3. But joy soon <u>effaced</u> every other feeling;. . . . .

   _____

4. "My principles were never trained, Jane: they may have grown a little <u>awry</u> for want of attention."

   _____

5. . . . .it told me of the alabaster cave and silver <u>vale</u> where we might live.

   _____

6. ". . . . if I had but a prospect of one day bringing Mr. Rochester an <u>accession</u> of fortune, I could better endure to be kept by him now."

   _____

7. . . . but on the whole I could see that he was excellently entertained; and that a lamb-like submission and turtle-dove sensibility, while fostering his <u>despotism</u> more, would have pleased his judgment, satisfied his common-sense, and even suited his taste, less.

   _____

Vocabulary - *Jane Eyre* - Chapters 24 - 26 Continued

8. "You puzzle me, Jane: your look and tone of sorrowful <u>audacity</u> perplex and pain me."

___

9. "Thank God!" he exclaimed, "that if anything <u>malignant</u> did come near you last night, it was only the veil that was harmed.---Oh, to think what might have happened!"

___

10. "I am in a condition to prove my allegation: an insuperable <u>impediment</u> to this marriage exists."

___

Part II: Determining the Meaning
    Match the vocabulary words to their dictionary definitions. If there are words for which you cannot figure out the definition by contextual clues and by process of elimination, look them up in a dictionary.

___ 49. acumen   A. caused to be unnoticed; wiped out; done away with
___ 50. allege   B. obstacle; hindrance; a physical defect
___ 51. effaced   C. amiss; wrong; a turn or twist to one side
___ 52. awry   D. evil in effect; malicious; deadly
___ 53. vale   E. mental acuteness; sharpness or keenness of insight
___ 54. accession   F. reckless boldness; daring; impudence
___ 55. despotism   G. valley
___ 56. audacity   H. to assert in argument; to declare as true but without proving
___ 57. malignant   I. addition or increase; attainment to an office, a right, or dignity
___ 58. impediment   J. absolute power or control; tyranny

Vocabulary - *Jane Eyre* - Chapters 27 - 29

Part I: Using Prior Knowledge and Contextual Clues

Below are the sentences in which the vocabulary words appear in the text. Read the sentence. Use any clues you can find in the sentence combined with your prior knowledge, and write what you think the underlined words mean on the lines provided.

1. But, then, a voice within me averred that I could do it; and foretold that I should do it.

_____

2. I saw that in another moment, and with one impetus of frenzy more, I should be able to do nothing with him.

_____

3. "And did you ever hear that my father was an avaricious, grasping man?"

_____

4. . . . even then I restrained myself: I eschewed upbraiding, I curtailed remonstrance; I tried to devour my repentance and disgust in secret; I repressed the deep antipathy I felt.

_____

5. . . . I had no presentiment of what it would be to me; no inward warning that the arbitress of my life--my genius for good or evil--waited there in humble guise.

_____

6. In the midst of my pain of heart, and frantic effort of principle, I abhorred myself.

_____

7 & 8. "Mortally: after all, it's tough work fagging away at a language with no master but a lexicon."

_____

_____

Vocabulary - *Jane Eyre* - Chapters 27 - 29 Continued

9. He said every nerve had been overstrained in some way, and the whole system must sleep torpid a while.

_____

10. When she left me, I felt comparatively strong and revived: ere long satiety of repose, and desire for action stirred me.

_____

Part II: Determining the Meaning
    Match the vocabulary words to their dictionary definitions. If there are words for which you cannot figure out the definition by contextual clues and by process of elimination, look them up in a dictionary.

___ 59. averred
___ 60. impetus
___ 61. avaricious
___ 62. eschewed
___ 63. arbitress
___ 64. abhorred
___ 65. fagging
___ 66. lexicon
___ 67. torpid
___ 68. satiety

A. working hard
B. a female who has the power to decide a point at issue
C. shunned; avoided; escaped
D. state of being surfeited with food or anything that satisfies desire; disgust or weariness caused by excess
E. affirmed; asserted as a fact
F. inactive; apathetic; dull
G. a dictionary; list of vocabulary words for a particular subject
H. greed of wealth; covetous
I. energy of motion; moving force; impulse
J. regarded with horror or repugnance; loathed

Vocabulary - *Jane Eyre* - Chapters 30 - 33

Part I: Using Prior Knowledge and Contextual Clues
Below are the sentences in which the vocabulary words appear in the text. Read the sentence. Use any clues you can find in the sentence combined with your prior knowledge, and write what you think the underlined words mean on the lines provided.

1. I am poor; for I find that, when I have paid my father's debts, all the <u>patrimony</u> remaining to me will be this crumbling grange. . . .

_____

2. I must not forget that these coarsely-clad little peasants are of flesh and blood as good as the <u>scions</u> of gentlest genealogy; and that the germs of native excellence, refinement, intelligence, kind feeling, are as likely to exist in their hearts as in those of the best-born.

_____

3. There was an enjoyment in accepting their simple kindness, and in repaying it by a consideration. . . . . .because, while it elevated them in their own eyes, it made them emulous to merit the <u>deferential</u> treatment they received.

_____

4. I know it is <u>ignoble</u>; a mere fever of the flesh: not, I declare, the convulsion of the soul.

_____

5. This was said with a careless, abstracted indifference, which showed that my solicitude was, at least in his opinion, wholly <u>superfluous</u>.

_____

6. "It seems her career there was very honorable: from a pupil, she became a teacher, like yourself--really it strikes me there are parallel points in her history and yours--she left it to be a governess; there, again, your fates were <u>analogous</u>; she undertook the education of the ward of a certain Mr. Rochester."

_____

Vocabulary - *Jane Eyre* - Chapters 30 - 33 Continued

7. What I want is, that you should write to your sisters and tell them of the fortune that has accrued to them.

_____

8. The instruments of transfer were drawn out: St. John, Diana, Mary, and I each became possessed of a competency.

_____

Part II: Determining the Meaning
   Match the vocabulary words to their dictionary definitions. If there are words for which you cannot figure out the definition by contextual clues and by process of elimination, look them up in a dictionary.

___ 69. patrimony
___ 70. scions
___ 71. deferential
___ 72. ignoble
___ 73. superfluous
___ 74. analogous
___ 75. accrued
___ 76. competency

A. descendants; shoots or twigs
B. not noble; inferior; of low character, aims, etc.
C. an income sufficient for ordinary wants
D. an estate inherited from one's father or ancestors
E. respectful; yielding to the opinion or will of another
F. increased; come as a natural product or result
G. unnecessary; excessive; more than is required
H. corresponding or comparable in some respect, though unlike as a whole

Vocabulary - *Jane Eyre* - Chapters 34 - 38

Part I: Using Prior Knowledge and Contextual Clues

Below are the sentences in which the vocabulary words appear in the text. Read the sentence. Use any clues you can find in the sentence combined with your prior knowledge, and write what you think the underlined words mean on the lines provided.

1. "No, Jane, no: this world is not the scene of fruition; do not attempt to make it so; nor of rest; do not turn slothful."

2. And while I smothered my paroxysm with all haste, he sat calm and patient, leaning on his desk and looking like a physician watching with the eye of science an expected and fully-understood crisis in a patient's malady.

3. "I say again, I will be your curate, if you like, but never your wife."

4. The late! I seemed to have received with full force, the blow I had been trying to evade.

5. He would have let the house: but could find no tenant, in consequence of its ineligible and insalubrious site.

6. "I thought you would be revolted, Jane, when you saw my arm, and my cicatrized visage."

7. "Yet how, on this dark and doleful evening, could you so suddenly rise on my lone hearth?"

8. He looked and spoke with eagerness: his old impetuosity was rising.

61

Vocabulary - *Jane Eyre* - Chapters 34 - 38 Continued

9. The coincidence struck me as too awful and <u>inexplicable</u> to be communicated or discussed.

_____

10. He had the advice of an <u>eminent</u> oculist; and he eventually recovered the sight of that one eye.

_____

Part II: Determining the Meaning
    Match the vocabulary words to their dictionary definitions. If there are words for which you cannot figure out the definition by contextual clues and by process of elimination, look them up in a dictionary.

___ 77. slothful   A. incapable of being explained
___ 78. malady   B. full of grief; sorrowful; gloomy
___ 79. curate   C. distinguished; high in rank, station or repute
___ 80. evade   D. sickness; bodily disorder or disease
___ 81. insalubrious   E. sudden or rash action; violence
___ 82. cicatrised   F. any ecclesiastic entrusted with the cure of souls; priest
___ 83. doleful   G. unfavorable to health
___ 84. impetuosity   H. elude; get away by dexterity or artifice
___ 85. inexplicable   I. scarred
___ 86. eminent   J. lazy; indolent; sluggish

ANSWER KEY - VOCABULARY
Jane Eyre

Chapters 1 - 6	Chapters 7 - 11	Chapters 12 - 16	Chapters 17 - 19
1. D	11. F	19. F	29. D
2. A	12. D	20. H	30. J
3. H	13. B	21. B	31. B
4. F	14. G	22. J	32. E
5. G	15. H	23. D	33. H
6. B	16. A	24. A	34. I
7. I	17. C	25. I	35. G
8. J	18. E	26. G	36. A
9. C		27. C	37. C
10. E		28. E	38. F

Chapters 20 - 23	Chapters 24 - 26	Chapters 27 - 29	Chapters 30 - 33
39. F	49. E	59. E	69. D
40. D	50. H	60. I	70. A
41. B	51. A	61. H	71. E
42. H	52. C	62. C	72. B
43. A	53. G	63. B	73. G
44. G	54. I	64. J	74. H
45. I	55. J	65. A	75. F
46. J	56. F	66. G	76. C
47. E	57. D	67. F	
48. C	58. B	68. D	

Chapters 34 - 38
77. J
78. D
79. F
80. H
81. G
82. I
83. B
84. E
85. A
86. C

DAILY LESSONS

LESSON ONE

Objectives
1. To introduce the *Jane Eyre* unit
2. To distribute books and other related materials--study guides, reading assignments, etc.
3. To preview the study questions for chapters 1-6
4. To familiarize students with the vocabulary for chapters 1-6
5. To read chapters 1-6

Activity #1

The introductory activity introduces the theme of individuality. Jane had her own values and her own goals, which made her a special person.

Have a guest speaker come in to discuss the importance of individuality--of having your own values and goals and how to find them if you don't have them.

Activity #2

Distribute the materials students will use in this unit. Explain in detail how students are to use these materials.

Study Guides Students should read the study guide questions for each reading assignment prior to beginning the reading assignment to get a feeling for what events and ideas are important in the section they are about to read. After reading the section, students will (as a class or individually) answer the questions to review the important events and ideas from that section of the book. Students should keep the study guides as study materials for the unit test.

Vocabulary Prior to reading a reading assignment, students will do vocabulary work related to the section of the book they are about to read. Following the completion of the reading of the book, there will be a vocabulary review of all the words used in the vocabulary assignments. Students should keep their vocabulary work as study materials for the unit test.

Reading Assignment Sheet You need to fill in the reading assignment sheet to let students know by when their reading has to be completed. You can either write the assignment sheet up on a side blackboard or bulletin board and leave it there for students to see each day, or you can "ditto" copies for each student to have. In either case, you should advise students to become very familiar with the reading assignments so they know what is expected of them.

Extra Activities Center The Extra Activities section of this unit contains suggestions for an extra library of related books and articles in your classroom as well as crossword and word search puzzles. Make an extra activities center in your room where you will keep these materials for students to use. (Bring the books and articles in from the library and keep several copies of the puzzles on hand.) Explain to students that these materials are available for students to use when they finish reading assignments or other class work early.

<u>Nonfiction Assignment Sheet</u> Explain to students that they each are to read at least one non-fiction piece from the in-class library at some time during the unit. Students will fill out a nonfiction assignment sheet after completing the reading to help you evaluate their reading experiences and to help the students think about and evaluate their own reading experiences.

<u>Books</u> Each school has its own rules and regulations regarding student use of school books. Advise students of the procedures that are normal for your school.

<u>Activity #3</u>
Preview the study questions and have students do the vocabulary work for Chapters 1-6 of *Jane Eyre*. Tell students that they should have this work completed and should complete reading chapters 1-6 prior to your next class meeting.

NONFICTION ASSIGNMENT SHEET
(To be completed after reading the required nonfiction article)

Name _____ Date _____

Title of Nonfiction Read _____

Written By _____ Publication Date _____

I. Factual Summary: Write a short summary of the piece you read.

II. Vocabulary
    1. With which vocabulary words in the piece did you encounter some degree of difficulty?

    2. How did you resolve your lack of understanding with these words?

III. Interpretation: What was the main point the author wanted you to get from reading his work?

IV. Criticism
    1. With which points of the piece did you agree or find easy to accept? Why?

    2. With which points of the piece did you disagree or find difficult to believe? Why?

V. Personal Response: What do you think about this piece? OR How does this piece influence your ideas?

LESSON TWO

Objectives
1. To review the main ideas and events from chapters 1-6
2. To preview the study questions and vocabulary for chapters 7-11
3. To read chapters 7-11
4. To give students practice reading orally
5. To evaluate students' oral reading

Activity #1

Give students a few minutes to formulate answers for the study guide questions for chapters 1-6 and then discuss the answers to the questions in detail. Write the answers on the board or overhead transparency so students can have the correct answers for study purposes. NOTE: It is a good practice in public speaking and leadership skills for individual students to take charge of leading the discussions of the study questions. Perhaps a different student could go to the front of the class and lead the discussion each day that the study questions are discussed during this unit. Of course, the teacher should guide the discussion when appropriate and be sure to fill in any gaps the students leave.

Activity #2

Give students about fifteen minutes to preview the study questions for chapters 7-11 of *Jane Eyre* and to do the related vocabulary work.

Activity #3

Have students read chapters 7-11 of *Jane Eyre* out loud in class. You probably know the best way to get readers with your class; pick students at random, ask for volunteers, or use whatever method works best for your group. If you have not yet completed an oral reading evaluation for your students this marking period, this would be a good opportunity to do so. A form is included with this unit for your convenience.

If students do not complete reading chapters 7-11 in class, they should do so prior to your next class meeting.

ORAL READING EVALUATION - *Jane Eyre*

Name _____ Class____ Date _____

SKILL	EXCELLENT	GOOD	AVERAGE	FAIR	POOR
Fluency	5	4	3	2	1
Clarity	5	4	3	2	1
Audibility	5	4	3	2	1
Pronunciation	5	4	3	2	1
_____	5	4	3	2	1
_____	5	4	3	2	1

Total _____   Grade _____

Comments:

LESSON THREE

Objectives
    1. To review the main events and ideas from chapters 7-11
    2. To preview the study questions for chapters 12-16
    3. To familiarize students with the vocabulary in chapters 12-16
    4. To read chapters 12-16

Activity #1
    Give students a few minutes to formulate answers for the study guide questions for chapters 4-8 and then discuss the answers to the questions in detail. Write the answers on the board or overhead transparency so students can have the correct answers for study purposes.

Activity #2
    Give students about fifteen minutes to preview the study questions for chapters 7-11 of *Jane Eyre* and to do the related vocabulary work.

Activity #3
    Have students read chapters 12-16 of *Jane Eyre* orally in class. Continue the oral reading evaluations.

    If students do not complete reading chapters 12-16 in class, they should do so prior to your next class meeting.

LESSON FOUR

Objectives
    1. To review the main events and ideas from chapters 12-16
    2. To preview the study questions for chapters 17-19
    3. To familiarize students with the vocabulary in chapters 17-19
    4. To read chapters 17-19

Activity #1
    Give students a few minutes to formulate answers for the study guide questions for chapters 12-16, and then discuss the answers to the questions in detail. Write the answers on the board or overhead transparency so students can have the correct answers for study purposes.

Activity #2
    Give students the remainder of the class period to do the prereading work for chapters 17-19 and to read those chapters silently.

    If students do not complete reading chapters 17-19 in class, they should do so prior to your next class meeting.

LESSON FIVE

Objectives
    1. To review the main events and ideas from chapters 17-19
    2. To preview the study questions for chapters 20-23 & 24-26
    3. To familiarize students with the vocabulary in chapters 20-23 & 24-26
    4. To read chapters 20-23 & 24-26

Activity #1
    Give students a few minutes to formulate answers for the study guide questions for chapters 17-19, and then discuss the answers to the questions in detail. Write the answers on the board or overhead transparency so students can have the correct answers for study purposes.

Activity #2
    Give students the remainder of the class period to do the prereading work for chapters 20-23 and 24-26 and to read those chapters silently.
    Tell students that they are to have this assignment completed by Lesson Seven. (Give students a day and a date.)

LESSON SIX

Objectives
1. To give students the opportunity to practice writing their personal opinions
2. To make an in-depth study of one of the characters (Jane or Rochester)
3. To give the teacher the opportunity to evaluate students' writing skills

Activity
Distribute Writing Assignment #1. Discuss the directions in detail and give students ample time to complete the assignment.

Follow-Up: After you have graded the assignments, have a writing conference with the students. (This unit schedules one in Lesson Eight.) After the writing conference, allow students to revise their papers using your suggestions and corrections. Give them about three days from the date they receive their papers to complete the revision. I suggest grading the revisions on an A-C-E scale (all revisions well-done, some revisions made, few or no revisions made). This will speed your grading time and still give some credit for the students' efforts.

LESSON SEVEN

Objectives
1. To check to see that students did the reading assignment
2. To evaluate students' understanding of the silent reading assignment
3. To preview the study questions and vocabulary for chapters 27-29
4. To read chapters 27-29

Activity #1
Quiz - Distribute quizzes and give students about 10 minutes to complete them. (NOTE: The quizzes may either be the short answer study guides or the multiple choice version.) Have students exchange papers. Grade the quizzes as a class. Collect the papers for recording the grades. (If you used the multiple choice version as a quiz, take a few minutes to discuss the answers for the short answer version if your students are using the short answer version for their study guides.)

Activity #2
Give students the remainder of the class period to do the prereading work for chapters 27-29 and to begin the reading assignment. Students should complete reading chapters 27-29 prior to Lesson Nine. (Give students a day and a date.)

WRITING ASSIGNMENT #1 - *Jane Eyre*

PROMPT
Jane is an unusual young woman, and Mr. Rochester is an unusual man. Your assignment is to choose to write about either Jane or Mr. Rochester and give your opinions about him or her so far in the novel. What do you think of her or him as a person?

PREWRITING
One way to begin is to decide whether you would rather write about Jane or Mr. Rochester. Then stop and think about his/her actions in the story. How does he or she relate to the other characters? What kind of a person is he or she? Jot down notes about your thoughts.

Look over your notes. If you could make only one statement about her or him to sum up what you think of his or her character, what would you say? Write it down in one sentence. This will be your thesis, the main idea of your paper.

What made you say that about the character? What were the reasons you said that? Write them down. Each reason will be the topic sentence for a paragraph supporting your thesis.

DRAFTING
Write an introductory paragraph in which you introduce your main idea, your thesis.

In the body of your composition, write one paragraph for each of the reasons/ideas you jotted down in the prewriting stage, using examples from the story to illustrate your point(s) to fill out your paragraphs.

Write a concluding paragraph in which you give your final thoughts and sum up your ideas.

PROMPT
When you finish the rough draft of your paper, ask a student who sits near you to read it. After reading your rough draft, he/she should tell you what he/she liked best about your work, which parts were difficult to understand, and ways in which your work could be improved. Reread your paper considering your critic's comments and make the corrections you think are necessary.

PROOFREADING
Do a final proofreading of your paper double-checking your grammar, spelling, organization, and the clarity of your ideas.

LESSON EIGHT

Objectives

    1. To give students the opportunity to practice using the resources of the library
    2. To give students some time to work on their nonfiction assignments
    3. To give students the opportunity to browse and read about topics that interest them
    4. To break up the reading-questions-answers routine

Activity

Take your students to the library. Tell them that the purpose of their being at the library is to find appropriate materials to complete the nonfiction reading assignment that goes along with this unit. Give students ample time to find materials and begin reading.

    Suggested topics:
        1. Supernatural events/dreams/visions
        2. Articles of criticism about *Jane Eyre*
        3. A biography of Charlotte Bronte
        4. English history
        5. Gothic or Victorian literature
        6. Moors
        7. Careers in education or art
        8. Famous artists and their works
        9. Philosophical importance of religion or education through history
        10. Important things to remember when choosing a spouse
        11. Marriage

LESSON NINE

Objectives

    1. To review the main events and ideas from chapters 27-29
    2. To preview the study questions for chapters 30-33
    3. To familiarize students with the vocabulary in chapters 30-33
    4. To read chapters 30-33

Activity #1

Give students a few minutes to formulate answers for the study guide questions for chapters 27-29, and then discuss the answers to the questions in detail. Write the answers on the board or overhead transparency so students can have the correct answers for study purposes.

Activity #2

Give students the remainder of the class period to do the prereading work for chapters 30-33 and to read those chapters silently. If students do not complete reading chapters 30-33 in class, they should do so prior to your next class meeting.

LESSON TEN

Objectives
1. To review the main ideas and events of chapters 30-33
2. To preview the study questions and vocabulary for chapters 34-38
3. To read chapters 34-38
4. To widen the breadth of students' knowledge about the topics discussed or touched upon in *Jane Eyre*
5. To check students' nonfiction reading assignments

Activity #1
Discuss the answers to the study guide questions for chapters 30-33. Write the answers on the board for students to copy down for study use later.

Activity #2
Ask each student to give a brief oral report about the nonfiction work he/she read for the nonfiction reading assignment. Your criteria for evaluating this report will vary depending on the level of your students. You may wish for students to give a complete report without using notes of any kind, or you may want students to read directly from a written report, or you may want to do something in between these two extremes. Just make students aware of your criteria in ample time for them to prepare their reports.

Start with one student's report. After that, ask if anyone else in the class has read about a topic related to the first student's report. If no one has, choose another student at random. After each report, be sure to ask if anyone has a report related to the one just completed. That will help keep a continuity during the discussion of the reports.

Activity #3
Tell students that they are to complete the vocabulary work and the reading for chapters 34-38 prior to Lesson Eleven. (Give students a day and a date.)

LESSON ELEVEN

Objectives
1. To review the main ideas and events from chapters 34-38
2. To discuss *Jane Eyre* on interpretive and critical levels

Activity #1
Take a few minutes at the beginning of the period to review the study questions for chapters 34-38.

Activity #2
Choose the questions from the Extra Discussion Questions/Writing Assignments which seem most appropriate for your students. A class discussion of these questions is most effective if students have been given the opportunity to formulate answers to the questions prior to the discussion. To this end, you may either have all the students formulate answers to all the questions, divide your class into groups and assign one or more questions to each group, or you could assign one question to each student in your class. The option you choose will make a difference in the amount of class time needed for this activity.

Activity #3
After students have had ample time to formulate answers to the questions, begin your class discussion of the questions and the ideas presented by the questions. Be sure students take notes during the discussion so they have information to study for the unit test.

EXTRA WRITING ASSIGNMENTS/DISCUSSION QUESTIONS - *Jane Eyre*

Interpretation

1. What are the main conflicts in the story and how are they resolved?

2. In what way is the setting important to the story?

3. From what point(s) of view is the story written.?

4. Where is the climax of the story? Justify your answer.

5. Which events in the novel are "turning points"--events which affect the course of the plot?

6. Is there any humor in the story? If so, where. If not, why not?

Critical

7. Compare and contrast the following characters:
   a. Jane/Blanche
   b. St. John/Mr. Rochester
   c. Eliza & Georgiana/Mary & Diana
   d. Miss Temple/Mrs. Fairfax
   e. Blanche/Rosamond
   f. Jane/Mr. Rochester
   g. Celene/Blanche
   h. Helen/Jane
   i. Bessie/Hannah
   j. Eliza/Georgiana
   k. Mary/Diana
   l. Bertha/Mrs. Reed

8. Explain the influence of each of the following people on Jane's life: Mrs. Reed, Miss Temple, Helen, Mr. Brocklehurst, St. John, Blanche, Mr. Mason, and John Eyre.

9. Characterize Charlotte Bronte's style of writing. How does it contribute to the value of the novel?

10. Is the story of *Jane Eyre* believable? Why or why not?

11. Do any of the characters change in the course of the novel? If so, who and how?

12. Are the characters in *Jane Eyre* stereotypes? Explain your answer.

Jane Eyre Extra Discussion Questions Page 2

13. Explain why Charlotte Bronte uses Jane to narrate the story.

14. Explain how Jane's appearance suits her personality

15. Jane thinks. Before she acts, before she speaks, she thinks. What basic principles guide her thoughts and judgements?

16. Explain how the ballad in chapter three relates to Jane.

17. In what ways is Jane set apart from the other characters in the book?

18. We don't meet Bertha until late in the story. What does she add to the story? What is the effect of her presence in the story?

19. Compare and contrast the physical buildings in which Jane lived during the time of the story.

Critical/Personal Response

20. What would Jane have done if she had discovered that Mr. Rochester had been killed in the fire which destroyed Thornfield?

21. Why, in this Victorian novel, was it imperative for someone to stop the marriage between Rochester and Jane?

Personal Response

22. Define the word "educated."

23. Would you have liked to have known Jane Eyre? Why or why not?

24. If you could be any of the characters in the book for a short time, which one would you choose? Why?

25. Did you enjoy reading *Jane Eyre*? Why or why not?

26. Jane had a definite set of values by which she led her life. Do you? What are they?

LESSON TWELVE

Objective
   To review all of the vocabulary work done in this unit

Activity
   Choose one (or more) of the vocabulary review activities listed below and spend your class period as directed in the activity. Some of the materials for these review activities are located in the Vocabulary Resource section of this unit.

VOCABULARY REVIEW ACTIVITIES

1. Divide your class into two teams and have an old-fashioned spelling or definition bee.

2. Give each of your students (or students in groups of two, three or four) a *Jane Eyre* Vocabulary Word Search Puzzle. The person (group) to find all of the vocabulary words in the puzzle first wins.

3. Give students a *Jane Eyre* Vocabulary Word Search Puzzle without the word list. The person or group to find the most vocabulary words in the puzzle wins.

4. Use a *Jane Eyre* Vocabulary Crossword Puzzle. Put the puzzle onto a transparency on the overhead projector (so everyone can see it), and do the puzzle together as a class.

5. Give students a *Jane Eyre* Vocabulary Matching Worksheet to do.

6. Divide your class into two teams. Use the *Jane Eyre* vocabulary words with their letters jumbled as a word list. Student 1 from Team A faces off against Student 1 from Team B. You write the first jumbled word on the board. The first student (1A or 1B) to unscramble the word wins the chance for his/her team to score points. If 1A wins the jumble, go to student 2A and give him/her a definition. He/she must give you the correct spelling of the vocabulary word which fits that definition. If he/she does, Team A scores a point, and you give student 3A a definition for which you expect a correctly spelled matching vocabulary word. Continue giving Team A definitions until some team member makes an incorrect response. An incorrect response sends the game back to the jumbled-word face off, this time with students 2A and 2B. Instead of repeating giving definitions to the first few students of each team, continue with the student after the one who gave the last incorrect response on the team. For example, if Team B wins the jumbled-word face-off, and student 5B gave the last incorrect answer for Team B, you would start this round of definition questions with student 6B, and so on. The team with the most points wins!

7. Have students write a story in which they correctly use as many vocabulary words as possible. Have students read their compositions orally! Post the most original compositions on your bulletin board.

LESSONS THIRTEEN AND FOURTEEN

Objectives
1. To further discuss the ideas presented in the book
2. To give students a chance to work together in small groups to exchange ideas and find information
3. To give students individual writing conferences

Activity #1

Divide your class into 9 groups - one group for each of the following topics:
1. Supernatural/dreams/visions
2. Religion
3. Education
4. Jane's artwork
5. Crime (or sin) and punishment
6. Appropriateness of names
7. Use of animals and animal imagery
8. Nature/weather
9. Conflicts and their resolutions

(NOTE: These are some suggestions for topics; feel free to add to or delete from this list.)

Students within the group should be assigned specific chapters in which to research the group's topic. Students should find any relevant passages and come to some reasonable conclusions about their topic as it relates to the book. One student in the group should be appointed secretary/spokesperson to write down and report the group's ideas.

Activity #2

Use the groups' work as a nucleus and a springboard for discussions about the major themes in the novel. Call on individual group members by chapter(s) to give the examples they found of their topic in those chapters. Jot them down briefly for students to copy into their notes. Ask the group spokesperson to give the group's thoughts about the theme development so far. Jot these down. Ask if anyone from the group has anything to add.

Take the time to discuss each theme thoroughly with the class and be sure to allow time for students (either members of the group or other class members) to express their ideas or ask questions.

NOTE: Having students report in this manner takes a little longer than having just one student from each group report, but it holds all group members accountable for their work.

Activity #3

While students are doing their group work, call individual students to your desk or some other private area where you can hold a writing conference to discuss students' first writing assignments. A Writing Evaluation Form is included for your convenience.

WRITING EVALUATION FORM - *Jane Eyre*

Name _____ Date _____

Grade _____

Circle One For Each Item:

Grammar:	corrections noted on paper
Spelling:	corrections noted on paper
Punctuation:	corrections noted on paper
Legibility:	excellent good fair poor
_____	excellent good fair poor

Strengths:

Weaknesses:

Comments/Suggestions:

LESSON FIFTEEN

Objectives
1. To give students the opportunity to practice writing to inform
2. To give students the chance to think in detail about *Jane Eyre*
3. To give the teacher a chance to evaluate students' individual writing
4. To give students the opportunity to correct their writing errors and produce an error-free paper

Activity

Distribute Writing Assignment #2. Discuss the directions orally in detail. Allow the remaining class time for students to complete the activity.

If students do not have enough class time to finish, the papers may be collected at the beginning of the next class period.

Follow-Up: Follow up as in Writing Assignment #1, allowing students to correct their errors and turn in the revision for credit. A good time for your next writing conferences would be the day following the unit test.

NOTE: After students have completed Writing Assignment #2, it is a fun activity to create videotaped segments of their reports, edit them together, and make a little film for review (and as more resource materials for your department for future classes of *Jane Eyre* readers to view).

WRITING ASSIGNMENT #2 - *Jane Eyre*

PROMPT
You have researched and discussed many different topics related to *Jane Eyre*. Your assignment is to consider *one* of the topics and write an informative report about it.

PREWRITING
Most of your prewriting has been done through prior research and class discussions. You should review your notes and choose a topic about which you would like to do this assignment.

After you decide on your topic, again review your notes relating to that topic. Pretend you are a reporter for a news magazine show and have been asked to cover this topic for a production next month. Decide what you would present and how you would present it. Make a little outline of the things you want to say in your report.

DRAFTING
As is the case with all compositions, your report should have a beginning (an introductory paragraph), a middle (the body of your report in which you state all of the information you want to convey), and an end (a concluding paragraph in which you give your final thoughts and sum up your information).

PROMPT
When you finish the rough draft of your paper, ask a student who sits near you to read it. After reading your rough draft, he/she should tell you what he/she liked best about your work, which parts were difficult to understand, and ways in which your work could be improved. Reread your paper considering your critic's comments and make the corrections you think are necessary.

PROOFREADING
Do a final proofreading of your paper double-checking your grammar, spelling, organization, and the clarity of your ideas.

LESSONS SIXTEEN AND SEVENTEEN

Objectives
    1. To bring the unit on *Jane Eyre* to a close
    2. To give students a visual representation of the story
    3. To set up and have a discussion comparing and contrasting the film version of the story with the written work

Activity #1
    Show a video of *Jane Eyre*. Tell students to make notes as they are watching the film, noting any variations in the plot, changes in characters, and any ways the film is different from the text of the novel.

Activity #2
    Hold a discussion about the similarities and differences between the book and the film and the differences between the film and students' expectations.

LESSON EIGHTEEN

Objectives
    1. To give students the opportunity to practice writing to express their own opinions
    2. To review the characters and events of the novel
    3. To give the teacher the opportunity to evaluate students' writing skills

Activity
    Distribute Writing Assignment #3. Discuss the directions in detail and give students this class period to work on the assignment.

WRITING ASSIGNMENT #3 - *Jane Eyre*

PROMPT

One of Charlotte Bronte's gifts was the ability to create interesting characters. *Jane Eyre* is quite a collection of personalities.

Your assignment is to write a composition in which you persuade your readers which character (besides Jane) is the most important character in the book.

PREWRITING

Write down the names of all the characters in the book. Stop and think about each one's role in the book and decide which one you think is the most important. Jot down your reasons for choosing that character. Next to your reasons, make a few notes about facts that support your reasons.

DRAFTING

Begin with an introductory paragraph in which you introduce the idea that _____ is the most important character in the book. Write one paragraph for each of your reasons for choosing that character using the facts that support your reasons to fill out the body of your paragraphs. Then write a concluding paragraph.

PROMPT

When you finish the rough draft of your paper, ask a student who sits near you to read it. After reading your rough draft, he/she should tell you what he/she liked best about your work, which parts were difficult to understand, and ways in which your work could be improved. Reread your paper considering your critic's comments and make the corrections you think are necessary.

PROOFREADING

Do a final proofreading of your paper double-checking your grammar, spelling, organization, and the clarity of your ideas.

LESSON NINETEEN

Objective
: To review the main ideas presented in *Jane Eyre*

Activity #1
: Choose one of the review games/activities included in this unit and spend your class period as outlined there. Some materials for these activities are located in the Unit Resource section of this unit.

Activity #2
: Remind students that the Unit Test will be in the next class meeting. Stress the review of the Study Guides and their class notes as a last-minute, brush-up review for homework.

REVIEW GAMES/ACTIVITIES - *Jane Eyre*

1. Ask the class to make up a unit test for *Jane Eyre*. The test should have 4 sections: matching, true/false, short answer, and essay. Students may use 1/2 period to make the test and then swap papers and use the other 1/2 class period to take a test a classmate has devised. (open book) You may want to use the unit test included in this packet or take questions from the students' unit tests to formulate your own test.

2. Take 1/2 period for students to make up true and false questions (including the answers). Collect the papers and divide the class into two teams. Draw a big tic-tac-toe board on the chalk board. Make one team X and one team O. Ask questions to each side, giving each student one turn. If the question is answered correctly, that students' team's letter (X or O) is placed in the box. If the answer is incorrect, no mark is placed in the box. The object is to get three marks in a row like tic-tac-toe. You may want to keep track of the number of games won for each team.

3. Take 1/2 period for students to make up questions (true/false and short answer). Collect the questions. Divide the class into two teams. You'll alternate asking questions to individual members of teams A & B (like in a spelling bee). The question keeps going from A to B until it is correctly answered, then a new question is asked. A correct answer does not allow the team to get another question. Correct answers are +2 points; incorrect answers are -1 point.

4. Have students pair up and quiz each other from their study guides and class notes.

5. Give students a *Jane Eyre* crossword puzzle to complete.

6. Divide your class into two teams. Use the *Jane Eyre* crossword words with their letters jumbled as a word list. Student 1 from Team A faces off against Student 1 from Team B. You write the first jumbled word on the board. The first student (1A or 1B) to unscramble the word wins the chance for his/her team to score points. If 1A wins the jumble, go to student 2A and give him/her a clue. He/she must give you the correct word which matches that clue. If he/she does, Team A scores a point, and you give student 3A a clue for which you expect another correct response. Continue giving Team A clues until some team member makes an incorrect response. An incorrect response sends the game back to the jumbled-word face off, this time with students 2A and 2B. Instead of repeating giving clues to the first few students of each team, continue with the student after the one who gave the last incorrect response on the team. For example, if Team B wins the jumbled-word face-off, and student 5B gave the last incorrect answer for Team B, you would start this round of clue questions with student 6B, and so on. The team with the most points wins!

UNIT TESTS

SHORT ANSWER UNIT TEST 1 - *Jane Eyre*

I. Matching

___ 1. Mr. Mason   A. One of Rochester's mistresses

___ 2. John Eyre   B. Eldest daughter of Mrs. Reed

___ 3. St. John   C. Jane thinks Rochester will marry her

___ 4. Mrs. Reed   D. Mr. Rochester's ward

___ 5. Celene Varens   E. Jane's special girlfriend at Lowood

___ 6. Mr. Rochester   F. Jane's teacher and idol at Lowood

___ 7. Eliza   G. Jane's uncle

___ 8. Blanche   H. Loses family fortune; kills himself

___ 9. Jane Eyre   I. Servant who cares for Bertha

___ 10. Mrs. Fairfax   J. Housekeeper at Thornfield

___ 11. Adele   K. Jane's uncle's widow; has custody of young Jane

___ 12. John Reed   L. Bertha's brother

___ 13. Helen   M. Servant at Gateshead

___ 14. Bessie   N. Benefactress of the Morton school

___ 15. Mr. Brocklehurst   O. Owns Thornfield; loves Jane

___ 16. Georgiana   P. Jane's cousin; missionary

___ 17. Miss Temple   Q. Rochester's insane wife

___ 18. Rosamond Oliver   R. Orphan who lives at Gateshead, Lowood, & Thornfield

___ 19. Grace Poole   S. Younger daughter of Mrs. Reed

___ 20. Bertha   T. Manager/treasurer of Lowood

Jane Eyre Short Answer Unit Test 1 Page 2

II. Short Answer
1. What is the significance of "Resurgam"?

2. How did Jane meet Mr. Rochester?

3. How did Jane react to her feelings of love for Mr. Rochester?

4. Why did Jane return to Gateshead?

5. What did the lightning-split tree foreshadow?

6. Why did Jane leave Thornfield?

7. Why did Jane reject St. John's proposal?

Jane Eyre Short Answer Unit Test Page 3

8. Why did Jane return to Thornfield after teaching at the Morton school?

9. What had happened at Thornfield in Jane's absence?

10. Explain how each of these names is appropriate:
    a. Gateshead:

    b. Lowood:

    c. Thornfield:

    d. Moor House:

    e. Ferndean:

Jane Eyre Short Answer Unit Test 1 Page 4

III. Essay

What is the point, the "moral of the story," of *Jane Eyre*? Be specific and use examples from the novel to support your answer.

Jane Eyre Short Answer Unit Test Page 5

IV. Vocabulary - Listen to the words and write them down. Go back later to fill in the correct definitions.

1.

2.

3.

4.

5.

6.

7.

8.

9.

10.

SHORT ANSWER UNIT TEST 2 - *Jane Eyre*

I. Matching

___ 1. Mr. Mason   A. Servant who cares for Bertha

___ 2. John Eyre   B. Jane thinks Rochester will marry her

___ 3. St. John   C. Servant at Gateshead

___ 4. Mrs. Reed   D. Housekeeper at Thornfield

___ 5. Celene Varens   E. Jane's cousin; missionary

___ 6. Mr. Rochester   F. Loses family fortune; kills himself

___ 7. Eliza   G. Eldest daughter of Mrs. Reed

___ 8. Blanche   H. Bertha's brother

___ 9. Jane Eyre   I. Rochester's insane wife

___ 10. Mrs. Fairfax   J. Mr. Rochester's ward

___ 11. Adele   K. Jane's uncle's widow; has custody of young Jane

___ 12. John Reed   L. Orphan who lives at Gateshead, Lowood & Thornfield

___ 13. Helen   M. Jane's uncle

___ 14. Bessie   N. Manager/treasurer of Lowood

___ 15. Mr. Brocklehurst   O. Younger daughter of Mrs. Reed

___ 16. Georgiana   P. Jane's teacher and idol at Lowood

___ 17. Miss Temple   Q. One of Rochester's mistresses

___ 18. Rosamond Oliver   R. Jane's special girlfriend at Lowood

___ 19. Grace Poole   S. Owns Thornfield; loves Jane

___ 20. Bertha   T. Benefactress of the Morton school

Jane Eyre Short Answer Unit Test 2 Page 2

II. Short Answer

1. Why do the Reeds treat Jane so unfairly?

2. What is the lifestyle of the girls at Lowood?

3. How is Jane's temperament different from Helen's?

4. How does Jane's visit with Miss Temple alter her thinking about Lowood?

5. Years after Helen's death, Jane has a stone marker with the word "Resurgam" carved upon it placed over Helen's grave. What is the significance of "Resurgam"?

6. How does Jane react to her feelings of love for Mr. Rochester?

7. Contrast Blanche and Jane.

8. Why does Jane consent to return to Gateshead?

Jane Eyre Short Answer Unit Test 2 Page 3

9. When Jane and Mr. Rochester profess their love and agree to marry, then a sudden storm breaks, resulting in lightning splitting the tree. What does nature reflect or foreshadow?

10. What "vision" does Jane have the night before her wedding?

11. Why were Jane and Mr. Rochester not married?

12. St. John and Jane both have strong wills; how are they different?

13. How is St. John, although wishing to do good in the world, a villain?

14. Contrast the manner in which St. John and Mr. Rochester seek to live.

15. How does the end of the novel represent typical Victorian expectations?

Jane Eyre Short Answer Unit Test 2 Page 4

III. Composition
    Explain the influence of each of these people on Jane's life:

a. Mrs. Reed

b. Miss Temple

c. Helen

d. St. John

e. John Eyre

Jane Eyre Short Answer Unit Test 2 Page 5

IV. Vocabulary

    Listen to the vocabulary word and spell it. After you have spelled all the words, go back and write down the definition.

1.

2.

3.

4.

5.

6.

7.

8.

9.

10.

KEY: SHORT ANSWER UNIT TESTS - *Jane Eyre*

The short answer questions are taken directly from the study guides.
If you need to look up the answers, you will find them in the study guide section.

Answers to the composition questions will vary depending on your
class discussions and the level of your students.

For the vocabulary section of the test, choose ten of the
words from the vocabulary lists to read orally for your students.

The answers to the matching section of the test are below.

Answers to the matching section of the Advanced Short Answer Unit Test
are the same as for Short Answer Unit Test #2.

<u>Test #1</u>
1. L
2. G
3. P
4. K
5. A
6. O
7. B
8. C
9. R
10. J
11. D
12. H
13. E
14. M
15. T
16. S
17. F
18. N
19. I
20. Q

<u>Test #2</u>
1. H
2. M
3. E
4. K
5. Q
6. S
7. G
8. B
9. L
10. D
11. J
12. F
13. R
14. C
15. N
16. O
17. P
18. T
19. A
20. I

ADVANCED SHORT ANSWER UNIT TEST - *Jane Eyre*

I. Matching

___ 1. Mr. Mason   A. Servant who cares for Bertha

___ 2. John Eyre   B. Jane thinks Rochester will marry her

___ 3. St. John   C. Servant at Gateshead

___ 4. Mrs. Reed   D. Housekeeper at Thornfield

___ 5. Celene Varens   E. Jane's cousin; missionary

___ 6. Mr. Rochester   F. Loses family fortune; kills himself

___ 7. Eliza   G. Eldest daughter of Mrs. Reed

___ 8. Blanche   H. Bertha's brother

___ 9. Jane Eyre   I. Rochester's insane wife

___ 10. Mrs. Fairfax   J. Mr. Rochester's ward

___ 11. Adele   K. Jane's uncle's widow; has custody of young Jane

___ 12. John Reed   L. Orphan who lives at Gateshead, Lowood & Thornfield

___ 13. Helen   M. Jane's uncle

___ 14. Bessie   N. Manager/treasurer of Lowood

___ 15. Mr. Brocklehurst   O. Younger daughter of Mrs. Reed

___ 16. Georgiana   P. Jane's teacher and idol at Lowood

___ 17. Miss Temple   Q. One of Rochester's mistresses

___ 18. Rosamond Oliver   R. Jane's special girlfriend at Lowood

___ 19. Grace Poole   S. Owns Thornfield; loves Jane

___ 20. Bertha   T. Benefactress of the Morton school

Jane Eyre Advanced Short Answer Unit Test Page 2

II. Short Answer
1. Explain the influence of each of the following people on Jane's life:
    a. Mrs. Reed

    b. Miss Temple

    c. Helen

    d. St. John

    e. John Eyre

2. Compare and contrast the following characters
    a. Jane & Blanche

    b. Helen & Jane

    c. Eliza & Georgiana

    d. St. John & Mr. Rochester

    e. Miss Temple & Mrs. Fairfax

Jane Eyre Advanced Short Answer Unit Test Page 3

3. We don't meet Bertha until late in the story. What does she add to the story? What is the effect of her presence on the story?

4. Jane thinks. Before she acts, before she speaks, she thinks. What basic principles guide her thoughts and her judgements?

5. Does Jane change any during the time of the story? If so, how? If not, why not?

Jane Eyre Advanced Short Answer Unit Test Page 4

III. Composition

Mary Ellen Snodgrass wrote, ". . . Jane Eyre demonstrates a strong need to be herself--to exercise her artistic talents, to take responsibility for her own actions, and to follow the dictates of a mature, developed sense of morality." Defend that statement.

Jane Eyre Advanced Short Answer Unit Test Page 5

IV. Vocabulary

Listen to the vocabulary words and write them down. After you have written down all the words, write a paragraph using all of the vocabulary words. The paragraph must in some way relate to *Jane Eyre*.

MULTIPLE CHOICE UNIT TEST 1 - *Jane Eyre*

I. Matching

___ 1. Mr. Mason   A. One of Rochester's mistresses

___ 2. John Eyre   B. Eldest daughter of Mrs. Reed

___ 3. St. John   C. Jane thinks Rochester will marry her

___ 4. Mrs. Reed   D. Mr. Rochester's ward

___ 5. Celene Varens   E. Jane's special girlfriend at Lowood

___ 6. Mr. Rochester   F. Jane's teacher and idol at Lowood

___ 7. Eliza   G. Jane's uncle

___ 8. Blanche   H. Loses family fortune; kills himself

___ 9. Jane Eyre   I. Servant who cares for Bertha

___ 10. Mrs. Fairfax   J. Housekeeper at Thornfield

___ 11. Adele   K. Jane's uncle's widow; has custody of young Jane

___ 12. John Reed   L. Bertha's brother

___ 13. Helen   M. Servant at Gateshead

___ 14. Bessie   N. Benefactress of the Morton school

___ 15. Mr. Brocklehurst O. Owns Thornfield; loves Jane

___ 16. Georgiana   P. Jane's cousin; missionary

___ 17. Miss Temple   Q. Rochester's insane wife

___ 18. Rosamond Oliver   R. Orphan who lives at Gateshead, Lowood & Thornfield

___ 19. Grace Poole   S. Younger daughter of Mrs. Reed

___ 20. Bertha   T. Manager/treasurer of Lowood

Jane Eyre Multiple Choice Unit Test 1 Page 2

II. Multiple Choice

1. What advice does Helen give Jane?
    A. Be quiet but sneaky.
    B. Fight back at every opportunity.
    C. Endure punishment and criticism and forgive and love the enemy.
    D. Go along with the rules, read, and assimilate as much knowledge as possible: then escape.

2. How is Jane's temperament different from Helen's?
    A. Jane is more religious.
    B. Jane is not as neat and organized as Helen.
    C. Jane is shy, but Helen is not.
    D. Jane is a fighter who cannot tolerate injustice.

3. How does Jane's visit with Miss Temple alter her thinking about Lowood?
    A. She begins to feel at home and with friends and feels good about her future.
    B. She dislikes it even more and feels even more depressed and hopeless.
    C. She looks at it as something that must be endured at all costs.
    D. She sees and understands the larger purpose of the school and appreciates what the administrators are trying to do--even if she doesn't like the way she personally is being treated.

4. What is the significance of "Resurgam"?
    A. It was the girls' school motto: that they would always remember one another and have a reunion every ten years.
    B. It was the word that Jane had engraved on the stone marker she placed on Helen's grave. It symbolized Helen's faith in the afterlife.
    C. It was part of a sermon that Brocklehurst gave to the girls every Sunday, reminding them that the consequences of their deeds, either good or bad, would follow them forever.
    D. It was a motivational message that Jane had made up for herself. Whenever she would get discouraged, she would remind herself that she had already come a long way, and could do more.

5. Bessie visits Jane and brings news from Gateshead. Which of the following statements is not one of the news items?
    A. Miss Eliza has spoiled Georgianna's elopement attempt.
    B. John Reed spends too much money and leads a dissipated life.
    C. Mrs. Reed has a mysterious illness and is confined to her room.
    D. A Mr. Eyre from Madeira came to see her but could not make the journey to Lowood because his ship was about to sail.

Jane Eyre Multiple Choice Unit Test 1 Page 3

6. How does Jane first meet Mr. Rochester?
    A. She is introduced at dinner by the housekeeper.
    B. Mr. Rochester observes her teaching Adele. He later calls her into his office and introduces himself.
    C. Mr. Rochester picks her up at the station when she first arrives.
    D. She meets him on the road from Hay while she is out walking. She helps him return to his saddle after his horse goes down on the ice.

7. How does Jane react to her feelings of love for Mr. Rochester?
    A. She denies them because she can't bear to be hurt.
    B. She talks to Mrs. Fairfax, who reminds her that Mr. Rochester is far above her station in life.
    C. She gives in to her feelings and begins to plan ways to attract Mr. Rochester even more.
    D. She frankly evaluates her plainness and social position and decides she has overreacted to his kindness.

8. What does Jane perceive in the relationship between Blanche and Mr. Rochester?
    A. She sees that they are deeply in love.
    B. She sees that Mr. Rochester loves Blanche, but she does not love him.
    C. She sees that Blanche's flirtatious arrows miss their mark, and Mr. Rochester does not love her.
    D. She sees that they both really despise the other but are playing the courting game for amusement.

9. What does Mr. Rochester ask of Jane on the night before he is to be married?
    A. He asks her to sit up with him.
    B. He asks her to pack his trunk.
    C. He asks her to have dinner with him.
    D. He asks her to stay in her room and not be seen.

10. Why does Jane consent to return to Gateshead?
    A. Mr. Rochester tells her she must do it, or she cannot stay at Thornfield.
    B. She knows it is the moral thing to do.
    C. She secretly hopes she will receive a portion of Mrs. Reed's fortune if she is kind and compassionate.
    D. She is merely curious about what all of the family members have been doing.

Jane Eyre Multiple Choice Unit Test 1 Page 4

11. When Jane and Mr. Rochester profess their love and agree to marry, a sudden storm breaks out. The resulting lightening splits the tree. What is this literary device called?
    A. Simile
    B. Personification
    C. Foreshadowing
    D. Transcendentalism

12. What "vision" does Jane have the night before the wedding?
    A. A ghost dressed in white, with a disfigured face, came into her room and ripped the wedding veil in half.
    B. The carriage overturned on the way to the church and she and Mr. Rochester were trapped under it.
    C. Thornfield was on fire and she was trapped upstairs.
    D. The church crumbled and fell apart just as they were ready to take their vows.

13. Who is guilty of setting the fire, ripping Jane's veil, and attacking Mason?
    A. Grace Poole
    B. Mr. Rochester
    C. Bertha
    D. Mrs. Fairfax

14. How does the author portray St. John's decision regarding Rosamond?
    A. He is correct in his rejection of her because their life dreams do not converge.
    B. He is making a foolish mistake because of his overly-zealous sense of mission.
    C. He is too concerned over the decision itself; it doesn't matter what the decision *is*, just as long as he makes a decision.
    D. He is acting too rashly and needs to consider the issue more carefully.

15. What is St. John's offer to Jane?
    A. He wants her to start a missionary church in Ireland.
    B. He wants her to take over the running of Moor House and open it as an orphanage.
    C. He wants to send her to school, all expenses paid.
    D. He wants her to come with him as his wife and companion missionary.

16. Which character in the novel looked for a meaning in a life of duty and self-denial?
    A. It was Jane Eyre.
    B. It was Mrs. Poole.
    C. It was Mr. Brocklehurst.
    D. It was St. John Rivers.

Jane Eyre Multiple Choice Unit Test 1 Page 5

17. The novel's conclusion is typical of the period: characters who did wrong must pay, those who acted with goodness are rewarded. What is the name of this period or style of writing?
    A. It is the Classical style.
    B. It is Realistic Fiction.
    C. It is the Victorian style.
    D. It is a tragedy.

Jane Eyre Multiple Choice Unit Test 1 Page 6

IV. Vocabulary: Multiple choice. Write in the letter of the word that matches the definition.

____ 1. ACCESSION   A. A female who has the power to decide an issue

____ 2. ITERATION   B. The face; appearance

____ 3. ACCRUED   C. Affirmed; asserted as a fact

____ 4. SUPERFLUOUS   D. Addition or increase; attainment to an office

____ 5. CONTUMELIOUS   E. Not noble; inferior

____ 6. EXECRATIONS   F. Humiliatingly insolent

____ 7. AVERRED   G. Drank

____ 8. ARBITRESS   H. Condition of being filled up with something

____ 9. AMELIORATED   I. Lazy; indolent; sluggish

____ 10. DEFERENTIAL   J. Respectful; yielding to the opinion or will of another

____ 11. VISAGE   K. Repetition

____ 12. REPLETION   L. Curses

____ 13. MALIGNANT   M. Unnecessary; more than is required

____ 14. PATRIMONY   N. Increased; come as a natural product or result

____ 15. IMBIBED   O. Nest of a bird of prey

____ 16. EYRIE   P. An estate inherited from one's father or ancestors

____ 17. SLOTHFUL   Q. Having wounded pride or self-esteem

____ 18. PIQUED   R. Devoted; unremittingly attentive

____ 19. IGNOBLE   S. Improved

____ 20. ASSIDUOUS   T. Evil in effect; malicious; deadly

MULTIPLE CHOICE UNIT TEST 2 - *Jane Eyre*

I. Matching

___ 1. Mr. Mason   A. Servant who cares for Bertha

___ 2. John Eyre   B. Jane thinks Rochester will marry her

___ 3. St. John   C. Servant at Gateshead

___ 4. Mrs. Reed   D. Housekeeper at Thornfield

___ 5. Celene Varens   E. Jane's cousin; missionary

___ 6. Mr. Rochester   F. Loses family fortune; kills himself

___ 7. Eliza   G. Eldest daughter of Mrs. Reed

___ 8. Blanche   H. Bertha's brother

___ 9. Jane Eyre   I. Rochester's insane wife

___ 10. Mrs. Fairfax   J. Mr. Rochester's ward

___ 11. Adele   K. Jane's uncle's widow; has custody of young Jane

___ 12. John Reed   L. Orphan who lives at Gateshead, Lowood & Thornfield

___ 13. Helen   M. Jane's uncle

___ 14. Bessie   N. Manager/treasurer of Lowood

___ 15. Mr. Brocklehurst   O. Younger daughter of Mrs. Reed

___ 16. Georgiana   P. Jane's teacher and idol at Lowood

___ 17. Miss Temple   Q. One of Rochester's mistresses

___ 18. Rosamond Oliver   R. Jane's special girlfriend at Lowood

___ 19. Grace Poole   S. Owns Thornfield; loves Jane

___ 20. Bertha   T. Benefactress of the Morton school

Jane Eyre Multiple Choice Unit Test 2 Page 2

II. Multiple Choice
1. What advice does Helen give Jane?
    A. Endure punishment and criticism and forgive and love the enemy.
    B. Go along with the rules, read, and assimilate as much knowledge as possible: then escape.
    C. Be quiet but sneaky.
    D. Fight back at every opportunity.

2. How is Jane's temperament different from Helen's?
    A. Jane is not as neat and organized as Helen.
    B. Jane is a fighter who cannot tolerate injustice.
    C. Jane is more religious.
    D. Jane is shy, but Helen is not.

3. How does Jane's visit with Miss Temple alter her thinking about Lowood?
    A. She looks at it as something that must be endured at all costs.
    B. She begins to feel at home and with friends and feels good about her future.
    C. She sees and understands the larger purpose of the school and appreciates what the administrators are trying to do--even if she doesn't like the way she personally is being treated.
    D. She dislikes it even more and feels even more depressed and hopeless.

4. What is the significance of "Resurgam"?
    A. It was part of a sermon that Brocklehurst gave to the girls every Sunday, reminding them that the consequences of their deeds, either good or bad, would follow them forever.
    B. It was a motivational message that Jane had made up for herself. Whenever she would get discouraged, she would remind herself that she had already come a long way and could do more.
    C. It was the girls' school motto: that they would always remember one another and have a reunion every ten years.
    D. It was the word that Jane had engraved on the stone marker she placed on Helen's grave. It symbolized Helen's faith in the afterlife.

5. Bessie visits Jane and brings news from Gateshead. Which of the following statements is not one of the news items?
    A. Mrs. Reed has a mysterious illness and is confined to her room.
    B. Miss Eliza has spoiled Georgiana's elopement attempt.
    C. A Mr. Eyre from Madeira came to see her but could not make the journey to Lowood because his ship was about to sail.
    D. John Reed spends too much money and leads a dissipated life.

Jane Eyre Multiple Choice Unit Test 2 Page 3

6. How does Jane first meet Mr. Rochester?
    A. Mr. Rochester observes her teaching Adele. He later calls her into his office and introduces himself.
    B. Mr. Rochester picks her up at the station when she first arrives.
    C. She meets him on the road from Hay while she is out walking. She helps him return to his saddle after his horse goes down on the ice.
    D. She is introduced at dinner by the housekeeper.

7. How does Jane react to her feelings of love for Mr. Rochester?
    A. She gives in to her feelings and begins to plan ways to attract Mr. Rochester even more.
    B. She frankly evaluates her plainness and social position and decides she has overreacted to his kindness.
    C. She talks to Mrs. Fairfax, who reminds her that Mr. Rochester is far above her station in life.
    D. She denies them because she can't bear to be hurt.

8. What does Jane perceive in the relationship between Blanche and Mr. Rochester?
    A. She sees that they both really despise the other but are playing the courting game for amusement.
    B. She sees that Mr. Rochester loves Blanche, but she does not love him.
    C. She sees that they are deeply in love.
    D. She sees that Blanche's flirtatious arrows miss their mark, and Mr. Rochester does not love her.

9. What does Mr. Rochester ask of Jane on the night before he is to be married?
    A. He asks her to pack his trunk.
    B. He asks her to stay in her room and not be seen.
    C. He asks her to sit up with him.
    D. He asks her to have dinner with him.

10. Why does Jane consent to return to Gateshead?
    A. She secretly hopes she will receive a portion of Mrs. Reed's fortune if she is kind and compassionate.
    B. She is merely curious about what all of the family members have been doing.
    C. She knows it is the moral thing to do.
    D. Mr. Rochester tells her she must do it or she cannot stay at Thornfield.

Jane Eyre Multiple Choice Unit Test 2 Page 4

11. When Jane and Mr. Rochester profess their love and agree to marry, a sudden storm breaks out. The resulting lightening splits the tree. What is this literary device called?
    A. Foreshadowing
    B. Simile
    C. Transcendentalism
    D. Personification

12. What "vision" does Jane have the night before the wedding?
    A. The carriage overturned on the way to the church, and she and Mr. Rochester were trapped under it.
    B. The church crumbled and fell apart just as they were ready to take their vows.
    C. Thornfield was on fire, and she was trapped upstairs.
    D. A ghost dressed in white, with a disfigured face, came into her room and ripped the wedding veil in half.

13. Who is guilty of setting the fire, ripping Jane's veil, and attacking Mason?
    A. Bertha
    B. Grace Poole
    C. Mr. Rochester
    D. Mrs. Fairfax

14. How does the author portray St. John's decision regarding Rosamond?
    A. He is too concerned over the decision itself; it doesn't matter what the decision *is*, just as long as he makes a decision.
    B. He is acting too rashly and needs to consider the issue more carefully.
    C. He is correct in his rejection of her because their life dreams do not converge.
    D. He is making a foolish mistake because of his overly-zealous sense of mission.

15. What is St. John's offer to Jane?
    A. He wants her to take over the running of Moor House and open it as an orphanage.
    B. He wants her to come with him as his wife and companion missionary.
    C. He wants to send her to school, all expenses paid.
    D. He wants her to start a missionary church in Ireland.

16. Which character in the novel looked for a meaning in a life of duty and self-denial?
    A. It was St. John Rivers.
    B. It was Mr. Brocklehurst.
    C. It was Jane Eyre.
    D. It was Mrs. Poole.

Jane Eyre Multiple Choice Unit Test 2 Page 5

17. The novel's conclusion is typical of the period: characters who did wrong must pay, those who acted with goodness are rewarded. What is the name of this period or style of writing?
    A. It is a tragedy.
    B. It is Realistic Fiction.
    C. It is the Classical style.
    D. It is the Victorian style.

Jane Eyre Multiple Choice Unit Test 2 Page 6

III. Vocabulary

____ 1. CURATE   A. The face; appearance

____ 2. IMPETUS   B. A whim; a fancy; a sudden change of mind

____ 3. PURLOINED   C. To disguise or conceal; excuse

____ 4. COMPETENCY   D. Stolen; done away with

____ 5. CAPRICE   E. Shunned; avoided; escaped

____ 6. INCARNATE   F. Any ecclesiastic intrusted with the care of souls

____ 7. INSALUBRIOUS   G. A pitcher

____ 8. COVERT   H. To embody in flesh; to represent in a concrete way

____ 9. PALLIATE   I. Circular; the eye; a sphere

____ 10. CONTUMELIOUS   J. Evil in effect; malicious; deadly

____ 11. CICATRIZED   K. Holder of an office; one who holds an ecclesiastical benefice; obligatory

____ 12. AFFABILITY   L. Unfavorable to health

____ 13. AUDACITY   M. Energy of motion; moving force; impulse

____ 14. VISAGE   N. An income sufficient for ordinary wants

____ 15. EWER   O. Humiliatingly insolent

____ 16. ORB   P. Friendliness; quality of being easy to talk with

____ 17. MALIGNANT   Q. A chat; talking together

____ 18. ESCHEWED   R. Disguised; secret; concealed

____ 19. INCUMBENT   S. Reckless boldness; daring; impudence

____ 20. CONFABULATION   T. Scarred

ANSWER SHEET - *Jane Eyre*
Multiple Choice Unit Tests

I. Matching
1. ___
2. ___
3. ___
4. ___
5. ___
6. ___
7. ___
8. ___
9. ___
10. ___
11. ___
12. ___
13. ___
14. ___
15. ___
16. ___
17. ___
18. ___
19. ___
20. ___

II. Multiple Choice
1. ___
2. ___
3. ___
4. ___
5. ___
6. ___
7. ___
8. ___
9. ___
10. ___
11. ___
12. ___
13. ___
14. ___
15. ___
16. ___
17. ___

IV. Vocabulary
1. ___
2. ___
3. ___
4. ___
5. ___
6. ___
7. ___
8. ___
9. ___
10. ___
11. ___
12. ___
13. ___
14. ___
15. ___
16. ___
17. ___
18. ___
19. ___
20. ___

ANSWER KEY - *Jane Eyre*
Multiple Choice Unit Tests

Answers to Unit Test 1 are in the left column. Answers to Unit Test 2 are in the right column.

I. Matching		II. Multiple Choice		IV. Vocabulary	
1. L	H	1. C	A	1. D	F
2. G	M	2. D	B	2. K	M
3. P	E	3. A	B	3. N	D
4. K	K	4. B	D	4. M	N
5. A	Q	5. C	A	5. F	B
6. O	S	6. D	C	6. L	H
7. B	G	7. D	B	7. C	L
8. C	B	8. C	D	8. A	R
9. R	L	9. A	C	9. S	C
10. J	D	10. B	C	10. J	O
11. D	J	11. C	A	11. B	T
12. H	F	12. A	D	12. H	P
13. E	R	13. C	A	13. T	S
14. M	C	14. A	C	14. P	A
15. T	N	15. D	B	15. G	G
16. S	O	16. D	A	16. O	I
17. F	P	17. C	D	17. I	J
18. N	T			18. Q	E
19. I	A			19. E	K
20. Q	I			20. R	Q

UNIT RESOURCE MATERIALS

BULLETIN BOARD IDEAS - *Jane Eyre*

1. Save one corner of the board for the best of students' *Jane Eyre* writing assignments.

2. Take one of the word search puzzles from the extra activities packet and with a marker copy it over in a large size on the bulletin board. Write the clue words to find to one side. Invite students prior to and after class to find the words and circle them on the bulletin board.

3. Title the board *Jane Eyre*: A NOVEL FULL OF CHARACTERS. Find pictures in magazines (or perhaps your library has a file of pictures) of people who look like the various characters in the novel. Place the picture on colorful paper, write the character's name under the picture (or next to it), and write a brief description of the character by it. You may wish to arrange these pictures on a genealogical table to show the relationships among the characters.

4. Divide the board into four sections: one each for Gateshead, Lowood, Thornfield, and Moor House. Place the names of the characters associated with each place within the appropriate section of the board. If you want to get fancy, you could design each space as the appropriate kind of "house," making Gateshead beautiful, Lowood institutional-like, Thornfield dark/gothic, and Moor House smaller, ordinary and cheerful.

5. Do a bulletin board about Victorian literature, listing the characteristics of Victorian Literature with several examples--little cut-out books showing the titles of several classic, Victorian novels with summaries of their plots inside.

6. Write several of the most significant quotations from the book onto the board on brightly colored paper.

7. Make a bulletin board listing the vocabulary words for this unit. As you complete sections of the novel and discuss the vocabulary for each section, write the definitions on the bulletin board. (If your board is one students face frequently, it will help them learn the words.)

EXTRA ACTIVITIES SECTION

One of the difficulties in teaching a novel is that all students don't read at the same speed. One student who likes to read may take the book home and finish it in a day or two. Sometimes a few students finish the in-class assignments early. The problem, then, is finding suitable extra activities for students.

The best thing I've found is to keep a little library in the classroom. For this unit on *Jane Eyre*, a biography of Charlotte Bronte would be interesting for some students. You can include other related books and articles about the supernatural, moors, philosophical importance of religion or education through history, careers in education or art, famous artists and their works, gothic or Victorian literature, or critics' articles about *Jane Eyre*.

Other things you may keep on hand are puzzles. We have made some relating directly to *Jane Eyre* for you. Feel free to duplicate them.

Some students may like to draw. You might devise a contest or allow some extra-credit grade for students who draw characters or scenes from *Jane Eyre*. Note, too, that if the students do not want to keep their drawings you may pick up some extra bulletin board materials this way. If you have a contest and you supply the prize (a CD or something like that perhaps), you could, possibly, make the drawing itself a non-returnable entry fee.

The pages which follow contain games, puzzles and worksheets. The keys, when appropriate, immediately follow the puzzle or worksheet. There are two main groups of activities: one group for the unit; that is, generally relating to the *Jane Eyre* text, and another group of activities related strictly to the *Jane Eyre* vocabulary.

Directions for these games, puzzles and worksheets are self-explanatory. The object here is to provide you with extra materials you may use in any way you choose.

MORE ACTIVITIES - *Jane Eyre*

1. Pick a chapter or scene with a great deal of dialogue and have the students act it out on a stage. (Perhaps you could assign various scenes to different groups of students so more than one scene could be acted and more students could participate.)

2. Use some of the related topics (noted earlier for an in-class library) as topics for research, reports or written papers, or as topics for guest speakers.

3. Have students keep a journal of their reactions to and thoughts about Jane's life. They should make an entry after each reading assignment.

4. Take short scenes from the novel. Assign parts in the scenes to various students (so that each student has a part). Students should memorize their lines and dress up as their characters to perform their scenes in front of the class in your classroom or on stage.

5. Have students design a book cover (front and back and inside flaps) for *Jane Eyre*.

6. Have students design a bulletin board (ready to be put up; not just sketched) for *Jane Eyre*.

7. In a class discussion, compare and contrast the principles set forth in *Jane Eyre* with the principles of our society today. Try to get students to vocalize what changes have happened since the Victorian era, and how those changes came about.

8. Have a missionary come and tell about his/her experiences.

9. Have students research the text to compile a list of duties of the servants and then create a "help wanted" advertisement for the position.

WORD SEARCH - *Jane Eyre*

All words in this list are associated with *Jane Eyre*. The words are placed backwards, forward, diagonally, up and down. The included words are listed below the word searches.

```
C O N S U M P T I O N E L P M E T R D K
X E T P Y J G S S L G R X A O H B O B R
Q Z L M G Z L M Q R Q E G Y P O O Y T V
F R E E D X W D R R U R O Y H W L E H K
X A M J N K Z S L Z U H X R O M R E W Z
M F I R Z E J S Y S B T E L G Y J G Y V
C I Y R R O C H E S T E R L E I W R L G
Y P L W F D M R X C N Z V N K L A P J P
Y G P L Z A Y G N P K Y H D S C T N Q K
P B X L C P X C K F Q O E N B N O J A G
G D Z B G O K G X V J K K K V Y J R C Q
K N C K R R T B X M C W S X H H S E B Y
J M E B J O E E F A K F A T Q S H F V T
M M N L E N N V T X I Z Z Y J C N B D R
H L G X E N K T I R I R L Z N O Q Y S V
D B E R T H A D E L E L I A R G H O S T
X E P V D M Y J E Y O K L Y Q Q L N G G
M O R T O N O S A M R B E S S I E E R T
```

ADELE	CONSUMPTION	JOHN EYRE	RED
ATTACKED	ELIZA	LIAR	REED
BERTHA	FAIRFAX	LOWOOD	RESURGAM
BESSIE	FIRE	MASON	ROCHESTER
BLANCHE	GEORGIANA	MILLCOTE	STJOHN
BROCKLEHURST	GHOST	MORTON	TEMPLE
BRONTE	HELEN	OLIVER	TREE
CELENE	JANE	POOLE	

CROSSWORD - *Jane Eyre*

CROSSWORD CLUES - *Jane Eyre*

ACROSS

1. Author
4. Housekeeper at Thornfield
8. Eldest daughter of Mrs. Reed
10. Mrs. Reed made Jane stay in the ___ room
11. Jane's teacher and idol at Lowood
14. Expectation or dream for the future
15. Mrs. ___; Jane's uncle's widow; has custody of young Jane
18. Also
19. Mr. Rochester's ward
20. Jane learned of the fire at Thornfield from the host at the inn in ___
22. Affirmative head gesture
23. Belonging to him
24. Jane's special friend at Lowood
29. Happiness
30. Servant at Gateshead
31. Helen's illness
34. Jane's cousin; missionary
37. Jane's uncle
38. Affirmative reply

DOWN

1. Jane thinks Rochester will marry her
2. Rosamond; Benefactress of the Morton school
3. Lightning split one after Jane & ___ Rochester decide to marry
5. Jane saved Mr. Rochester from the ___
6. Brocklehurst called Jane a ___
7. Manager/treasurer at Lowood ___
9. Mr. Mason was ___ by Bertha
12. St. John found a job for Jane at ___ School for Girls
13. ___ Institution; charity school for orphaned girls
16. Purely bad
17. Extreme dislike
20. Mr. ___; Bertha's brother
21. One of Rochester's mistresses
25. A little bad; disobedient or mischievous
26. Jane saw one ripping her wedding veil
27. Rochester's insane wife
28. Means 'I shall rise again'
32. Grace; servant who cares for Bertha
33. Things to eat
35. Orphan who lives at Gateshead, Lowood & Thornfield
36. Coordinating conjunction

CROSSWORD ANSWER KEY - *Jane Eyre*

B	R	O	N	T	E			F	A	I	R	F	A	X			
L		L		R		L					I					B	
A		I		E	L	I	Z	A			R	E	D		B	R	
N		V		E		A		T	E	M	P	L	E		H	O	P	E
C		E				R		T		O		O				C	
H		R	E	E	D			A		R		W		H		K	
E				V				C		T	O	O		A	D	E	L	E
				I				K		O		O		T		E	
	M	I	L	L	C	O	T	E		N	O	D		E		H	I	S
	A			E		D										U	
	S		H	E	L	E	N				G		B		R		R
J	O	Y		E		A				H		B	E	S	S	I	E
	N		C	O	N	S	U	M	P	T	I	O	N		R		T	S
			E		G		O			S		T					U
		F			H		O	S	T	J	O	H	N				R
		O		A		T		L		A		A					G
		J	O	H	N	E	Y	R	E			N					A
		D		D				Y	E	S						M	

131

MATCHING QUIZ/WORKSHEET 1 - *Jane Eyre*

____ 1. ST. JOHN   A. Means 'I shall rise again'

____ 2. HELEN   B. Rochester's insane wife

____ 3. RED   C. Jane's cousin; missionary

____ 4. BROCKLEHURST   D. One of Rochester's mistresses

____ 5. BERTHA   E. Rosamond; Benefactress of the Morton school

____ 6. ELIZA   F. Author

____ 7. JOHN EYRE   G. Mrs. ___; Jane's uncle's widow; has custody of young Jane

____ 8. RESURGAM   H. Manager/treasurer at Lowood

____ 9. CELENE   I. Jane's uncle

____ 10. MORTON   J. Jane's special friend at Lowood

____ 11. FIRE   K. Mrs. Reed made Jane stay in the ___ room

____ 12. TEMPLE   L. St. John found a job for Jane at ___ School for Girls

____ 13. GHOST   M. Lightning split one after Jane & Rochester decide to marry

____ 14. BESSIE   N. Servant at Gateshead

____ 15. TREE   O. Mr. ____; Bertha's brother

____ 16. POOLE   P. Jane saw one ripping her wedding veil

____ 17. MASON   Q. Grace; servant who cares for Bertha

____ 18. BRONTE   R. Jane saved Mr. Rochester from the ___

____ 19. OLIVER   S. Eldest daughter of Mrs. Reed

____ 20. REED   T. Jane's teacher and idol at Lowood

MATCHING QUIZ/WORKSHEET 2 - *Jane Eyre*

____ 1. RED	A. ___ Institution; charity school for orphaned girls

____ 2. CONSUMPTION	B. Helen's illness

____ 3. TREE	C. Jane thinks Rochester will marry her

____ 4. BERTHA	D. Means 'I shall rise again'

____ 5. FIRE	E. One of Rochester's mistresses

____ 6. LIAR	F. Jane's teacher and idol at Lowood

____ 7. JANE	G. Jane's uncle

____ 8. REED	H. Rochester's insane wife

____ 9. OLIVER	I. Mrs. ___; Jane's uncle's widow; has custody of young Jane

____ 10. CELENE	J. Jane saved Mr. Rochester from the ___

____ 11. LOWOOD	K. Orphan who lives at Gateshead, Lowood & Thornfield

____ 12. JOHNEYRE	L. Servant at Gateshead

____ 13. ADELE	M. Rosamond; Benefactress of the Morton School

____ 14. MASON	N. Mrs. Reed made Jane stay in the ___ room

____ 15. POOLE	O. Mr. ____; Bertha's brother

____ 16. BLANCHE	P. Grace; servant who cares for Bertha

____ 17. RESURGAM	Q. Younger daughter of Mrs. Reed

____ 18. GEORGIANA	R. Mr. Rochester's ward

____ 19. BESSIE	S. Lightning split one after Jane & Rochester decide to marry

____ 20. TEMPLE	T. Brocklehurst called Jane a ___

KEY: MATCHING QUIZ/WORKSHEETS - *Jane Eyre*

Worksheet 1	Worksheet 2
1. C	1. N
2. J	2. B
3. K	3. S
4. H	4. H
5. B	5. J
6. S	6. T
7. I	7. K
8. A	8. I
9. D	9. M
10. L	10. E
11. R	11. A
12. T	12. G
13. P	13. R
14. N	14. O
15. M	15. P
16. Q	16. C
17. O	17. D
18. F	18. Q
19. E	19. L
20. G	20. F

JUGGLE LETTER REVIEW GAME CLUE SHEET - *Jane Eyre*

SCRAMBLED	WORD	CLUE
TREBNO	BRONTE	Author
DER	RED	Mrs. Reed made Jane stay in the ___ room
OLDOWO	LOWOOD	Institution; charity school for orphaned girls
RAIL	LIAR	Brocklehurst called Jane a ___
ISMTONOUNCP	CONSUMPTION	Helen's illness
GRERMASU	RESURGAM	Means 'I shall rise again'
RIFE	FIRE	Jane saved Mr. Rochester from the ___
ERET	TREE	Lightning split one after Jane & Rochester decide to marry
SHOGT	GHOST	Jane saw one ripping her wedding veil
TEDACATK	ATTACKED	Mr. Mason was ___ by Bertha
RONTOM	MORTON	St. John found a job for Jane at ___ School for Girls
LOMILTEC	MILLCOTE	Jane learned of the fire at Thornfield from the host at the inn in ___
SANMO	MASON	Mr. ___; Bertha's brother
NEROHEJY	JOHNEYRE	Jane's uncle
TOJNHS	ST. JOHN	Jane's cousin; missionary
DERE	REED	Mrs. ___; Jane's uncle's widow; has custody of young Jane
LEENCE	CELENE	One of Rochester's mistresses
HEROTERCS	ROCHESTER	Owns Thornfield; loves Jane
AZLIE	ELIZA	Eldest daughter of Mrs. Reed
LACEHBN	BLANCHE	Jane thinks Rochester will marry her
ENAJ	JANE	Orphan who lives at Gateshead, Lowood & Thornfield
RAXAFFI	FAIRFAX	Housekeeper at Thornfield
DEELA	ADELE	Mr. Rochester's ward
NEEHL	HELEN	Jane's special friend at Lowood
SEIBES	BESSIE	Servant at Gateshead
KLOBHETRRCUS	BROCKLEHURST	Manager/treasurer at Lowood
OEGGANAIR	GEORGIANA	Younger daughter of Mrs. Reed
PLMEET	TEMPLE	Jane's teacher and idol at Lowood
ROVILE	OLIVER	Rosamond; Benefactress of the Morton school
LOOPE	POOLE	Grace; servant who cares for Bertha
RATEBH	BERTHA	Rochester's insane wife

VOCABULARY RESOURCE MATERIALS

VOCABULARY WORD SEARCH - *Jane Eyre*

```
L K J J T X S E V X E M Z T N S Y G M A L Y D X
E S C I O N F Y W Y P L P I O Z T N L Q E T S L
A M E L I O R A T E D M A L A D Y L E X I C O N
H S L Z F N T I D I R F A V E E E N E M B R Z H
S H S L S N C A D Y S C C Z E G N C I S U R Z C
H U K I E A V U M E E O I L E R R S A M B C O Q
V C O N D E M S M T W R U L U A R R C F O N A G
P P I U S U Y G A B T E B T T F D E G O F N K B
L M A S L X O R I A E O H I E O H D D A N E G P
E D I N O F U U C N N O C N P E T B M I C Y I
P L H R O C R I S G E N T I S R M U O R R S E I
B A A T Y I C E I V S X C P E E L I Y L U J M D
D P L R S U T E P M I C P T A A C E P O S P S A
M O W L B A V A C U O S S L T T P I G I E P C G
Q A L Z I I T I T V S E A I I I R O R D Q R W T
Y P D E S A T I E U U C O G T C L I I P I U O H
W Z Q N F E T R E Q P N I H E A A M M M A R E S
W Y E Y C U T E E T Y M E O N J E B O O P C B D
B P Y S Q X L S W S Y T I A N N B N L I N Q W A
S L A I T N E R E G S N W V T S Y M D E K Y P M
```

ABRIDGE	EFFACED	LEXICON
ACRIMONY	EMINENT	MALADY
ACUMEN	ENIGMAS	PALLIATE
ALLEGE	ENSCONCED	PAROXYSM
AMELIORATED	EPITHET	PATRIMONY
ANALOGOUS	ESCHEWED	PIQUED
ARBITRESS	EWER	RUTH
ASCETIC	FAIN	SARDONIC
ASSIDUOUS	IGNOBLE	SATIETY
AUDACITY	IGNOMINY	SCIONS
BLISS	IMPEDIMENT	SEQUESTERED
CICATRIZED	IMPETUOSITY	SLOTHFUL
CONFABULATION	IMPETUS	SOLACE
COVERT	IMPUTATION	SUPERFLUOUS
CURATE	INCUMBENTLY	TORPID
DOLEFUL	INEXPLICABLE	VALE
		VISAGE

VOCABULARY CROSSWORD - *Jane Eyre*

VOCABULARY CROSSWORD CLUES - *Jane Eyre*

ACROSS
2. Mental acuteness; sharpness of insight
4. A whim; a fancy; a sudden change of mind
8. A pitcher
9. Opposite of right; went away
10. Supreme happiness
12. Nest of a bird of prey
13. Corresponding or comparable in some respect although unlike as a whole
14. Elude; get away by dexterity or artifice
16. Irritating or angry sharpness
17. Sight organ
18. Riddles; puzzles; mysteries
19. Valley
21. Look with your eyes
24. Willingly; gladly by preference
25. Respectful; yielding to the opinion or will of another
26. Take action
27. Sorrow; regret; pity or compassion
28. Happy; cheerful; lighthearted
29. Destroy
30. Increased; come as a natural product or result
34. An estate inherited from one's father or ancestors
35. Negative reply
36. State of being overfilled
37. Mr. ____; Bertha's brother
40. Mrs. Reed made Jane stay in the ___ room
42. Author
43. Addition or increase; attainment to an office
45. Jane saved Mr. Rochester from the ___
47. Myself
48. The face; appearance
49. Affirmative response
50. Regarded with horror or repugnance; loathed

DOWN
1. Amiss; wrong; a turn or twist to one side
2. A female who has the power to decide an issue
3. Distinguished of being explained
4. Any ecclesiastic intrusted with the care of souls
5. Not noble; inferior
6. To declare as true but without proving
7. Friendliness; quality of being easy to talk with
11. Devoted; unremittingly attentive
13. Affirmed; asserted as a fact
15. Obstacle; hindrance; a physical defect
16. One who practices religious austerities; a hermit
20. Greedy; covetous
22. Absolute power or control; tyranny
23. Repetition
24. Working hard
30. Omit; shorten; curtail; deprive of
31. Willful and obstinate resistance or disobedience
32. Opposite of closed
33. Disguised; secret; concealed
36. Descendants; shoots or twigs
38. Mr. Rochester's ward
39. Lightning split one after Jane & Rochester decide to marry
41. Brocklehurst called Jane a ___
44. Circular; the eye; a sphere
46. That's all; there is no more; the --

VOCABULARY CROSSWORD ANSWER KEY - *Jane Eyre*

				A		A	C	U	M	E	N			C	A	P	R	I	C	E
A	A			E	W	E	R		M					U				G		
L	E	F	T		R		B	L	I	S	S			R				N		A
L		F		E	Y	R	I	E		N		A	N	A	L	O	G	O	U	S
E	V	A	D	E			T		I		E		V		T			B		S
G		B			A	C	R	I	M	O	N	Y		E	Y	E		L		I
E	N	I	G	M	A	S		E		P		T		R		V	A	L	E	D
		L			C		S	E	E		D		R		I		V			U
F	A	I	N		E		S		D	E	F	E	R	E	N	T	I	A	L	D O
A		T		R	U	T	H		I		S		D		E		R			U
G	A	Y			I			M		P			R	U	I	N				S
G				A	C	C	R	U	E	D		O		A		C		C		
I				B		O		N		T		P	A	T	R	I	M	O	N	Y
N	O			R		N		T		I		E		I		O		V		
G		S	A	T	I	E	T	Y		M	A	S	O	N		O		U	E	A
		C		D		U		T		M			N		S		R	E	D
		I		G		M		R					L			T			E
B	R	O	N	T	E	A	C	C	E	S	S	I	O	N		F	I	R	E	
	N				C		E			R			A		N	M	E		
V	I	S	A	G	E	Y	E	S			A	B	H	O	R	R	E	D		

142

VOCABULARY WORKSHEET 1 - *Jane Eyre*

____ 1. Respectful; yielding to the opinion or will of another
      A. Ignominy   B. Deferential   C. Visage   D. Orb

____ 2. Bitter; scornful or mocking
      A. Sardonic   B. Pensive   C. Ignoble   D. Slothful

____ 3. Intangible; cannot be grasped by the mind
      A. Inexplicable   B. Execrations   C. Exonerated   D. Ewer

____ 4. Caused to be unnoticed; wiped out; done away with
      A. Ameliorated   B. Effaced   C. Bliss   D. Meager

____ 5. Unfavorable to health
      A. Satiety   B. Insalubrious   C. Ewer   D. Vale

____ 6. To declare as true but without proving
      A. Contumelious   B. Malady   C. Competency   D. Allege

____ 7. Energy of motion; moving force; impulse
      A. Purloined   B. Competency   C. Palliate   D. Impetus

____ 8. Holder of an office; one who holds an ecclesiastical benefice; obligatory
      A. Incumbent   B. Presentiments   C. Fain   D. Covert

____ 9. A female who has the power to decide an issue
      A. Indolence   B. Arbitress   C. Patrimony   D. Allege

____ 10. Affirmed; asserted as a fact
      A. Edification   B. Competency   C. Despotism   D. Averred

____ 11. Condition of being filled up with something
      A. Presentiments   B. Repletion   C. Prerogatives   D. Piqued

____ 12. A chat; talking together
      A. Deferential   B. Confabulation   C. Impetuosity   D. Vale

____ 13. Irritating or angry sharpness
      A. Ensconced   B. Acrimony   C. Doleful   D. Meager

____ 14. One who practices religious austerities; a hermit
      A. Iteration   B. Affability   C. Enigmas   D. Ascetic

____ 15. Instruction in moral improvement or benefit
      A. Covert   B. Edification   C. Sequestered   D. Evade

____ 16. Any ecclesiastic entrusted with the care of souls
      A. Ascetic   B. Contumacy   C. Curate   D. Palliate

____ 17. Willingly; gladly by preference
      A. Fain   B. Edification   C. Insalubrious   D. Imbibed

____ 18. Lazy; indolent; sluggish
      A. Fagging   B. Evade   C. Slothful   D. Piqued

____ 19. Incapable of being explained
      A. Affability   B. Inexplicable   C. Competency   D. Ascetic

____ 20. Supreme happiness
      A. Solace   B. Accession   C. Deferential   D. Bliss

VOCABULARY WORKSHEET 2 - *Jane Eyre*

____ 1. EVADE   A. Elude; get away by dexterity or artifice

____ 2. ORB   B. Unnecessary; more than is required

____ 3. PATRIMONY   C. Bitter; scornful or mocking

____ 4. MALIGNANT   D. Basely treacherous; deliberately faithless

____ 5. LEXICON   E. A charge or insinuation of something discreditable

____ 6. FAIN   F. Not noble; inferior

____ 7. AVARICIOUS   G. Regarded with horror or repugnance; loathed

____ 8. EMINENT   H. Willful and obstinate resistance or disobedience

____ 9. ACRIMONY   I. Greedy; covetous

____ 10. IGNOBLE   J. Distinguished

____ 11. CONTUMACY   K. Curses

____ 12. SARDONIC   L. Irritating or angry sharpness

____ 13. IMPEDIMENT   M. A dictionary

____ 14. EPITHET   N. A name; a term applied to a person or thing to express an attribute

____ 15. ACCESSION   O. An estate inherited from one's father or ancestors

____ 16. IMPUTATION   P. Circular; the eye; a sphere

____ 17. PERFIDIOUS   Q. Evil in effect; malicious; deadly

____ 18. SUPERFLUOUS R. Addition or increase; attainment to an office

____ 19. EXECRATIONS S. Willingly; gladly by preference

____ 20. ABHORRED   T. Obstacle; hindrance; a physical defect

KEY: VOCABULARY WORKSHEETS - *Jane Eyre*

Worksheet 1	Worksheet 2
1. B	1. A
2. A	2. P
3. A	3. O
4. B	4. Q
5. B	5. M
6. D	6. S
7. D	7. I
8. A	8. J
9. B	9. L
10. D	10. F
11. B	11. H
12. B	12. C
13. B	13. T
14. D	14. N
15. B	15. R
16. C	16. E
17. A	17. D
18. C	18. B
19. B	19. K
20. D	20. G

VOCABULARY JUGGLE LETTER REVIEW GAME CLUES - *Jane Eyre*

SCRAMBLED	WORD	CLUE
EBDOARRH	ABHORRED	Regarded with horror or repugnance; loathed
BIDEGRA	ABRIDGE	Omit; shorten; curtail; deprive of
CSIANCSOE	ACCESSION	Addition or increase; attainment to an office
UCADECR	ACCRUED	Increased; come as a natural product or result
NROCIAYM	ACRIMONY	Irritating or angry sharpness
EUCNMA	ACUMEN	Mental acuteness; sharpness of insight
FIYTAFBAIL	AFFABILITY	Friendliness; quality of being easy to talk with
LEEAGL	ALLEGE	To declare as true but without proving
ERAMIEDAOTL	AMELIORATE	Improved
AULNSAOOG	ANALOGOUS	Corresponding or comparable in some respect although unlike as a whole
TPNAHTYAI	ANTIPATHY	Instinctive opposition; natural dislike; aversion
BSASRIRTE	ARBITRESS	A female who has the power to decide an issue
IEACSTC	ASCETIC	One who practices religious austerities; a hermit
UDOSASISU	ASSIDUOUS	Devoted; unremittingly attentive
CDAYUATI	AUDACITY	Reckless boldness; daring; impudence
RIUOCAISAV	AVARICIOUS	Greedy; covetous
ERDVREA	AVERRED	Affirmed; asserted as a fact
WYAR	AWRY	Amiss; wrong; a turn or twist to one side
IBSLS	BLISS	Supreme happiness
PIAECRC	CAPRICE	A whim; a fancy; a sudden change of mind
AZDCERICTI	CICATRIZED	Scarred
COPTNYCMEE	COMPETENCY	An income sufficient for ordinary wants
NBIOUCFLTAAON	CONFABULATION	A chat; talking together
TMUCAOYCN	CONTUMACY	Willful and obstinate resistance or disobedience

UEICTONOMLSU	CONTUMELIOUS	Humiliatingly insolent
ETVROC	COVERT	Disguised; secret; concealed
AUETCR	CURATE	Any ecclesiastic intrusted with the care of souls
FETLNEIAERD	DEFERENTIAL	Respectful; yielding to the opinion or will of another
EDOMSITPS	DESPOTISM	Absolute power or control; tyranny
LLFODEU	DOLEFUL	Full of grief; sorrowful; gloomy
EIATOFNDICI	EDIFICATION	Instruction in moral improvement or benefit
FCAEFDE	EFFACED	Caused to be unnoticed; wiped out; done away with
INEMNTE	EMINENT	Distinguished
GASNEIM	ENIGMAS	Riddles; puzzles; mysteries
SOEECNCDN	ENSCONCED	Settled securely or snugly
HIPTETE	EPITHET	A name; a term applied to a person or thing to express an attribute
CEDEWEHS	ESCHEWED	Shunned; avoided; escaped
VDEAE	EVADE	Elude; get away by dexterity or artifice
EREW	EWER	A pitcher
XCATOERISNE	EXECRATIONS	Curses
OEAXENRDET	EXONERATED	Relieved from an obligation; freed from blame
REYEI	EYRIE	Nest of a bird of prey
GGNIFGA	FAGGING	Working hard
NAFI	FAIN	Willingly; gladly by preference
GNBIOEL	IGNOBLE	Not noble; inferior
NYIMINOG	IGNOMINY	Disgrace; dishonor; public contempt
MBEBIDI	IMBIBED	Drank
LIAPBLEMPA	IMPALPABLE	Intangible; cannot be grasped by the mind
PIENTIEMDM	IMPEDIMENT	Obstacle; hindrance; a physical defect
EUMPTOIYTIS	IMPETUOSITY	Sudden or rash action; violence
TISUMPE	IMPETUS	Energy of motion; moving force; impulse
MTNOIAIUTP	IMPUTATION	A charge or insinuation of something discreditable
ARINETNCA	INCARNATE	To embody in flesh; to represent in a concrete way
ICETNMNUB	INCUMBENT	Holder of an office; one who holds an ecclesiastical benefice; obligatory
DECIONELN	INDOLENCE	Laziness
ILICBELAXNEP	INEXPLICABLE	Incapable of being explained
SURUSANLBIOI	INSALUBRIOUS	Unfavorable to health
TRNIOITAE	ITERATION	Repetition

IOXCLEN	LEXICON	A dictionary
LDMAYA	MALADY	Sickness; bodily disorder or disease
GNTAINALM	MALIGNANT	Evil in effect; malicious; deadly
EREMAG	MEAGER	Lean; deficient in quantity or quality
BRO	ORB	Circular; the eye; a sphere
LALTPIEA	PALLIATE	To disguise or conceal; excuse
XSAMPOYR	PAROXYSM	Sudden, violent outburst; a convulsion; fit of emotion
TIYNOAMRP	PATRIMONY	An estate inherited from one's father or ancestors
PSEVEIN	PENSIVE	Deeply, seriously or sadly thoughtful
RMPOEPRLIYTE	PEREMPTORILY	Positive in speech, manner, tone; dictatorial
FDEOSPIIUR	PERFIDIOUS	Basely treacherous; deliberately faithless
IUQDEP	PIQUED	Having wounded pride or self-esteem
EOTSEVAPRGIR	PREROGATIVES	Prior or exclusive rights or privileges
RNISTNESTMEEP	PRESENTIMENTS	Forebodings; feelings that something is going to happen
PODENILRU	PURLOINED	Stolen; done away with
ARETNMI	RAIMENT	Clothing
ELIPERNOT	REPLETION	Condition of being filled up with something
UTHR	RUTH	Sorrow; regret; pity or compassion
CISNODRA	SARDONIC	Bitter; scornful or mocking
YATIETS	SATIETY	State of being overfilled
INCSOS	SCIONS	Descendants; shoots or twigs
EDESUSERTQE	SEQUESTERED	Secluded; withdrawn from others
OHULSLFT	SLOTHFUL	Lazy; indolent; sluggish
ALCSEO	SOLACE	Something that gives comfort or consolation
UEFSPUOSULR	SUPERFLUOUS	Unnecessary; more than is required
RDOTIP	TORPID	Inactive; apathetic; dull
LVEA	VALE	Valley
IGEASV	VISAGE	The face; appearance